Please return/renew this item by the last date shown on this label, or on your self-service receipt.

To renew this item, visit **www.librarieswest.org.uk** or contact your library

Your borrower number and PIN are required.

Libraries

D1419319

4 4 0097831 2

HOW TO BE GOOD

GOOD

or How to Be Moral and Virtuous in a Wicked World

GARY COX

BLOOMSBURY ACADEMIC

LONDON • NEW YORK • OXFORD • NEW DELHI • SYDNEY

BLOOMSBURY ACADEMIC
Bloomsbury Publishing Plc
50 Bedford Square, London, WC1B 3DP, UK
1385 Broadway, New York, NY 10018, USA

BLOOMSBURY, BLOOMSBURY ACADEMIC and the Diana logo are trademarks of
Bloomsbury Publishing Plc

First published in Great Britain 2020

Handshake graphic © DenPotisev / Getty Images
Heart graphic © Ulimi / Getty Images

Bloomsbury Publishing Plc does not have any control over, or responsibility for,
any third-party websites referred to or in this book. All internet addresses given
in this book were correct at the time of going to press. The author and publisher
regret any inconvenience caused if addresses have changed or sites have
ceased to exist, but can accept no responsibility for any such changes.

A catalogue record for this book is available from the British Library.

A catalog record for this book is available from the Library of Congress.

ISBN: PB: 978-1-3501-5459-9
       ePDF: 978-1-3500-6837-7
       eBook: 978-1-3500-6839-1

Typeset by RefineCatch Limited, Bungay, Suffolk
Printed and bound in Great Britain

To find out more about our authors and books visit www.bloomsbury.com
and sign up for our newsletters.

CONTENTS

ACKNOWLEDGEMENTS

Many thanks to moral philosophers I have known personally at the universities of Southampton, Birmingham and Bristol, particularly Professor Nicholas Dent for his rigorous reading of the first draft of this book and his excellent advice on how to improve it. Thanks also to friends and family, particularly Sharon, for their encouragement and support.

1
WHAT IS GOODNESS?

Goodness and Being Good

There is a belief, particularly within the Roman Catholic Church, that certain rare persons are so full of goodness that when they die their bodies do not rot. They are held to be *incorrupt*, a sure sign that they are a saint, an exceptionally good and holy person with a hotline to God who will be formally declared a saint (canonized) in due course.

In Fyodor Dostoyevsky's epic novel *The Brothers Karamazov* (1880), the death of the renowned holy man Zosima is expected to be followed by the miracle of his *incorruption*. Instead, his rotting corpse soon stinks to high heaven. Some take this as a sign that he was not so holy after all, others as a symbol of what he consistently taught, that the body and the physical world are without value, that it is only what belongs to the world of the spirit that matters: kindness, forgiveness, goodness and the love of God.

If you ate a saint would you taste and consume the goodness in him or her, as you are said by wholefood fanatics to taste and consume the goodness in organic vegetables fresh from the garden? Well, I have never tried it – the most we have of saints in a physical sense is dry, dusty bones and perhaps a covering of parchment-like flesh that would make a poor soup – but it seems highly unlikely that eating a saint is a way of acquiring goodness.

Many people have believed, and some people still believe, that goodness is a quasi-physical property of saints, a property that can be possessed by owning some part of them or some object closely linked to them, some religious relic, like St Peter's sandals. But this is silly, superstitious, fetishistic thinking, the belief that certain objects are haunted by magical powers through association.

We only have to ask ourselves in what did the goodness of a certain saint really consist, what was it that made him a saint, apart from the Catholic Church canonizing him? Did he just sit around being good, radiating his goodness out of his halo, glowing all over with an aura of altruism? Even religious people who believe that a saint must have a very good soul within him, brimming over with the God-given glitter of goodness and all that bling, would probably concede that the true goodness of a saint really consists in the way he lived his life, in the good lessons that he taught, in the good deeds that he performed and in the many good ways that he actively helped, encouraged and comforted others.

Goodness, then, is not really a physical property of saints or anyone else, not even a very vaporous one, but a certain way of behaving, a pattern of behaviour, that if it is adopted with sufficient consistency by someone, it can correctly be said of them, of their character, 'He/she is a good person.' Saying they are a good person means they have consistently *acted* in a certain exemplary manner in the right spirit and for the best purposes and can be expected to continue to do so, not that the blessed light of goodness literally shines out of them.

Thanks to all my talk about saints you will have already realized that I am talking about *moral goodness* rather than about being good at football or maths. When we think a person is morally good – whatever moral goodness is exactly – we allow ourselves to say, 'He is good.' When watching Cristiano Ronaldo play football we might also say, 'He is good', and everyone understands, in context, that we mean he is a good footballer, not that he is a good person, although, of course, Ronaldo may also be a good person.

Anyway, if Ronaldo is a good person, it is not because he is a good footballer, any more than he is a good person because he is a good-looking guy. Psychologists tell us that people often make the mistake of assuming that a person must be morally good because they are good-looking, which kind of takes us back to the mistaken belief that goodness is some sort of physical property.

In Jane Austen's psychologically and ethically penetrating novel *Sense and Sensibility* (1811), Mrs Dashwood and her daughter Marianne, governed as they are by emotion, jump to the conclusion that John Willoughby must be a highly virtuous person simply because he is handsome and dashing. Elinor, Mrs Dashwood's oldest daughter, is wise enough to realize that virtue does not consist in such superficial and transitory qualities. Her suspicions that Willoughby lacks any real moral fibre are eventually proven to be correct when he shows himself to be unreliable, inconsiderate and self-seeking in his treatment of poor, innocent, naive, passionate Marianne, who nearly dies of a broken heart as a result of his selfishness.

> 'The whole of his behaviour,' replied Elinor, 'from the beginning to the end of the affair, has been grounded on selfishness. It was selfishness which first made him sport with your affections; which afterwards, when his own were engaged, made him delay the confession of it, and which finally carried him from Barton. His own enjoyment, or his own ease, was, in every particular, his ruling principle.'
>
> *Sense and Sensibility*, p. 327

Willoughby is somewhat redeemed towards the end of the novel when he reveals with genuine remorse that his actions were driven by mere weakness rather than villainy. But, then, most of the evil in the world stems from mundane human weakness, stupidity and lack of consideration rather than from deeply devilish desires. As Hannah Arendt, a philosopher who narrowly escaped the Nazis is 1941, points out, evil is so often *banal*. Arendt coined the phrase 'the banality of evil' in her 1963 book *Eichmann in Jerusalem: A Report on the Banality of Evil*.

Although good looks alone should not be taken as a sign of moral goodness, the ancient Greeks often argued that looking after one's health and appearance to the best of one's ability without succumbing to vanity, and developing and maintaining one's physique so that it is athletic, are all part of achieving personal *arête* (excellence). *Arête* for the ancient Greeks referred to excellence of any kind, the excellence of a meal, the excellence of a horse, but it also meant *moral virtue*. Certainly, the opposite, damaging one's health and appearance through overindulgence or neglect, was considered a vice. This example reveals that goodness is partly to do with how we treat ourselves, even if the greater part of it is to do with how we treat others.

From the outset, it can be said that goodness, morality, ethics has an awful lot to do with our behaviour as it relates to other people, but you already knew that. This book is certainly 'introducing' you to something you very likely already know quite a lot about, even if you have never before thought about your everyday understanding of ethics, your common-sense awareness of right and wrong, in any kind of systematic, analytical, philosophical manner.

So, we tend to distinguish between *being good*, as in being a morally good person, and *being good at*, as in being good at football. However, to what extent is being a morally good person also actually about being good at something? To what extent is being morally good a skill, a craft, even an art? And if it is a skill, can it be learnt? Surely all skills can be learnt to a lesser or greater extent. If it is a skill, can it be learnt from reading this book? Well, yes and no.

This book hopefully sheds a fair amount of light on what it is to be morally good, which is a start, but *knowing* what it is to be morally good is just not the same as being morally good. To be morally good one has to put one's knowledge into practice. Only in its exercise does a skill really exist, only through practice does a skill develop rather than deteriorate.

A person, Willoughby for example, can know what they ought to do in a certain situation in order to do the right thing, and yet still not do it, perhaps because they are selfish or spiteful or simply weak-willed. In his great work on ethics, *The Nicomachean Ethics* (349 BCE), the ancient Greek philosopher Aristotle, star pupil of Plato and teacher of Alexander the Great, argues that *akrasia* – weakness of will or lack of self-control – is a highly undesirable character trait as it undermines all our best intentions. Interestingly, to *cease* to be *akratic* requires a strong will, and that is precisely the problem of overcoming it.

Akrasia is sometimes translated as *incontinence*, a term more commonly used these days to mean lack of voluntary control over urination and/or defecation. If you have ever needed the loo really badly, and who has not, you will be aware of the enormous amount of *continence* – self-control – required to avoid incontinence. The Roman poet Ovid perfectly summed up the nature of incontinence – in the moral, non-medical sense – when he said, '*Video meliora proboque, deteriora sequor*': 'I see the better course and approve, and yet I follow the worse' (*Metamorphoses*, Book VII, 20).

Still, having said all that, and even lapsed into Latin in order to say it, my hope is that the knowledge of moral goodness acquired from reading this book will at least set some readers, including you personally, on the road towards righteousness and virtue. Hopefully, reading this book will encourage you to reflect more deeply than perhaps you have in the past on your general behaviour and how it affects others. Hopefully, this philosophical reflection will in turn inspire you to modify your behaviour for the better. If you are not morally perfect already that is.

Alternatively, there is a very real danger that the more you learn about ethics, the less ethical you may become, especially if you end up concluding, as many have, that there is actually no such thing as right and wrong, that morality is all just smoke and mirrors, mere *subjective* approval or disapproval pretending to be something more factual and substantial.

I feel obliged to say at this point, in order to get it out of the way as early as possible, that this book is not in the business of advising you to live as I do. I am myself no paragon of moral virtue and do not hold myself up as an example to follow. I am not a lifestyle guru projecting himself as a role model of how to live; I leave that to the leaders of various religious cults and the conceited celebrities who follow them.

I dare say I am not a bad person as bad people go. I have, for example, never murdered anyone. But neither am I the kindest, most helpful, most charitable person that I know. I believe I am, like most people, somewhere in the middle on the saint–sinner scale. I believe that what I know about morality from a philosophical point of view has helped me to be a better person to some extent, but my knowledge also reminds me that I could do much better, which perhaps makes me far more of a sinner than I like to think.

Perhaps I should be out there doing good deeds rather than sitting in writing this book, walking the walk rather than just talking the talk. Then again, if this book encourages some people towards greater goodness then it will prove to be a good deed in itself, a whole series of them in fact. But what if, as already suggested, this book encourages some people towards greater badness? Hold on, surely the nub of that suggestion was that there may actually be no such thing as right and wrong, in which case it is not actually possible for anyone to be good or bad at all.

Goodness and God

The view that goodness and badness are mere illusions, even delusions, is a relatively modern notion, one that has emerged in Western thinking as the influence of religion has declined. A few hundred years ago, when nobody seriously doubted God's existence, morality was, in a sense, a far less complicated matter. Quite simply, to act morally, to be good, was to do God's will as defined by the Bible and the Church. To act immorally, to be bad, was to defy God.

In 'Morality and Religion' (1998) H. O. Mounce takes the example of the ancient Hebrew attitude to the Ten Commandments. Nowadays, we tend to view the first four commandments as setting out our religious duties to God, and the remaining six as setting out our moral duties to our neighbours. The ancient Hebrews, however, made no such distinction and saw all Ten Commandments as concerned with our duties to God. As Mounce says, 'Thus the last six do not instruct us in how to serve our neighbour as distinct from serving God. Rather they instruct us in how God wishes us to serve him in our dealings with our neighbour' ('Morality and Religion', in *Philosophy of Religion: A Guide to the Subject*, p. 253).

The story of Moses receiving the Ten Commandments from God on tablets of stone (Exodus 20) illustrates in a graphic and unsophisticated way that is easily grasped the perceived unity of morality and divine will. For people who take the Bible literally, which in the past was just about everyone, there can be no clearer illustration that it is God's will that gives meaning to moral concepts such as duty and justice.

As to *why* you damn well ought to obey God's will, what in the jargon we might call 'the *force* of moral imperatives', that was seen, and is still seen by some, to derive from the promise of rewards and the threat of punishments to be dealt out by God in an afterlife. If you have been good enough in your life, obedient enough to God, then you go to heaven; if you have been particularly bad, particularly disobedient to God, then you go to hell.

Without God, so the argument goes, moral rules would lack authority. There would be no ultimate sanction against doing evil, no reason to do good. Indeed, without God, so the argument goes, no distinction between good and bad behaviour could be made. Life would be a free-for-all where anything goes. Everything would be permitted.

As this book proceeds, many reasons to be good will emerge other than desire for eternal paradise and fear of eternal damnation, reasons that place value on goodness for what it can achieve in *this* life, rather than for what it can achieve, and avoid, in the next.

In any event, there is a serious problem with goodness and morality being whatever God wills. If what is good is whatever God wills then whatever God wills is good. God could will anything he liked and it would still be good. But God would not do that, religious people say. He would not decide the nature of goodness and badness on a whim, making it up as he goes along, he is just too good for that.

This argument, however, immediately establishes that what is good must be something independent of God. If what is good is not defined by God's caprice then it must be defined by certain *independent* moral principles that God, in his goodness and wisdom, chooses to follow. God knows that if he does not follow these principles then what he wills, or rather advocates and enforces, will not actually be good. The question now arises as to which is higher, God or morality? It would appear that morality is higher, as its principles *dictate* what God *must* do, at least if he is to be a morally good God.

The dilemma that arises from considering which is higher, God or morality, was first identified by the ancient Greeks. It has come to be known as the *Euthyphro dilemma* or the *Euthyphro question* because it was first explored in detail in Plato's dialogue *Euthyphro* (c. 399–395 BCE).

Socrates and Euthyphro meet near the law courts of ancient Athens where Euthyphro is pressing murder charges against his own father. Euthyphro believes himself to be an expert on religion and ethics. However, in the ensuing debate on the nature of piety (holiness), Socrates employs his usual method of rigorous questioning – *Socratic method* – to hog-tie poor Euthyphro in the constricting knots of his own contradictions. Thus, Euthyphro's claim to ethical expertise is rubbished and his ignorance exposed. Socrates nails the Euthyphro dilemma with these famous words: 'We shall soon be better able to judge, my good sir. Consider this question: is what is pious loved by the gods because it is pious, or is it pious because it is loved?' (Plato, *Euthyphro*, 9a–10b, p. 31).

In 399 BCE, only a few weeks after his meeting with Euthyphro is supposed to have taken place, Socrates was unjustly executed by the Athenian state for impiety and corrupting the young. Socrates' penchant for exposing the ignorance of the movers and shakers of ancient Athens made him powerful enemies. It is a wonder, therefore, that the many leading Athenian citizens he irritated and humiliated over the years with his smart-arsed *reductio ad absurdum* did not throttle him to death with their own bare hands long before he was finally made to drink the deadly poison hemlock.

It must be noted that it is debatable whether or not Socrates was actually *made* to drink the poison. He was given plenty of chances to abscond, which he declined to take, and drank the poison himself rather than it being poured down his throat by force. Some scholars have even argued that Socrates committed suicide. Nonetheless, it was the machinations of the Athenian state against Socrates that broadly speaking led to his death and certainly Plato, Socrates' great friend and follower, places ultimate responsibility for his demise upon the Athenian state.

The Euthyphro dilemma exposes serious difficulties with the key religious claim that God is all powerful, the supreme being and so on, for how can God be all powerful if moral principles constitute a power over him? I shall not explore these difficulties further in this book, as an excursion into the heady realms of theology would take us too far away from our current concerns. If these difficulties stir your curiosity, however, and you would like to know more about them, then try my book *The God Confusion* (2013) which explores them in detail.

While on the subject of God and morality, however, we do need to explore the phenomenon of *conscience*, be it real or imagined. Moral conscience, most often though not always believed to be God-given, has played a huge role down through the centuries in people's thinking about goodness and badness and is, therefore, very much part of our current concerns.

It is still widely believed that the sense of right and wrong that governs most people's thoughts and actions, that causes them to suffer guilt and anxiety or to enjoy peace of mind, can only have been bestowed upon them by a divine being that is the very essence of moral goodness. Conscience, indeed, is still seen by some to be the voice of God within us, an inner angel telling us what we *ought* to do, and in the past virtually everyone saw conscience this way.

It is, however, highly doubtful that conscience is the God-given moral compass that it has long been characterized as. To begin with, some people clearly do not have a conscience. Psychopaths and sociopaths commit atrocities without experiencing any sense of shock or remorse whatsoever. 'His pulse never got over eighty-five, even when he ate her tongue' (*The Silence of the Lambs*, comment on the fictional serial killer Hannibal Lecter).

If conscience is God-given then surely God would have the power to make sure everyone had one. Admittedly, this is not the strongest argument against conscience because it can be countered that everyone has a conscience but that it is possible to ignore it, or that evil forces can so quieten the voice of a person's inner angel that it cannot be heard.

The real problem with conscience is its characterization as an *infallible* inner capacity for distinguishing right from wrong. There were Nazis who believed so sincerely in the rightness of the extermination programme that they saw carrying it out as a matter of conscience, and actually suffered pangs of guilt and anxiety if they failed to meet their genocidal quota. If conscience was an infallible, inner, God-given capacity to distinguish right from wrong then surely it could not make such terrible mistakes. We are able to identify those Nazis who acted on conscience as morally mistaken and confused because, it seems, we are able to apply *objective moral standards* in judging them.

Arguably, if there were no objective moral standards, only the *subjective* standard of conscience, then a person might feel himself forced to the absurd conclusion that what the Nazis did was morally right because their consciences deemed it to be so. Of course, a person would not feel himself forced to this conclusion if it is not one of the subjective standards of *his* conscience that if someone else follows *their* conscience then that is fine by him. Such are the peculiarities that arise in the absence of objective moral standards.

We have yet to investigate what objective moral standards there are of course, what they are, where they come from and on what they are based. But stress not, the crucially important investigation into those standards forms the greater part of this goodness guide going forward.

So, conscience itself cannot be the measure of what is right and wrong. Indeed, there is really no such thing as conscience as traditionally understood. The sense of right and wrong that many people undoubtedly have is not an innate, God-given capacity, but arguably something that is acquired through reason, experience, socialization and education. Its sources are down to earth, empirical and/or rational, not otherworldly and metaphysical.

If people are generally disposed or even predisposed to goodness, to being good, to behaving morally, this is not because they have a God-given conscience, but because acting morally, acting with some degree of consideration for others, more often than not serves their physical and emotional needs as evolved social animals.

So, just as goodness cannot be whatever conscience says it is, so goodness cannot be whatever God says it is. If 'X is good because God wills it' then we are led to the absurd conclusion that doing good is, as J. L. Mackie says in his influential book *Ethics: Inventing Right and Wrong* (1977, p. 230), 'merely prudent but slavish conformity to the arbitrary demands of a capricious tyrant'. The only sensible answer to the Euthyphro question, although it raises certain theological difficulties, is the one that the great German philosopher Immanuel Kant argues for in his *Critique of Practical Reason* (1788): 'God wills x because it is good.'

To conclude that 'God wills x because it is good' has the important consequence of revealing moral principles and values to be as independent of God as mathematical principles and values. Morality is revealed as autonomous, as a phenomenon that can be studied without reference to God and religion. Moreover, removing religious superstition from the picture contributes significantly to the clarification of certain contentious moral issues such as abortion, which is considered in Chapter 4: 'Goodness at Issue'.

Recognizing that morality is autonomous allows goodness to be identified with the best ways to live as human social animals, rather than with the best ways to serve God. Removing God from the sphere of the ethical allows morality to be seen, not as a set of commandments delivered from on high, as something imposed on humankind from outside, but as a *functional device*, a phenomenon that has evolved along with human intelligence and civilization for the purposes of ensuring many of the most basic and vital requirements of social life.

Arguably, morality functions very much like the rules of a game, regulating the 'game' of human social life and enabling it to proceed. Indeed, along with habit and custom, with which it is closely bound, morality enables social life to exist, to the extent that there could be no social life without it. As I argue in more detail in my conclusion, human social life and ethics are no more separable than football and the rules of football. It is revealing that the term *ethics* is derived from the ancient Greek term *ethikos*, which is closely related to the term *ethos*, meaning 'habit or custom'.

Goodness and Philosophy

By way of concluding this opening chapter, this rather choppy boat trip around the Cape of Good Ness designed to give you the kind of glimpse of Mount Morality that makes you keen to scale her sides and discover more, I want to ponder why it is that philosophers are so interested in goodness, badness, rightness, wrongness, moral conduct, moral issues and the whole sometimes mind-bending ethical caboodle. Hopefully, this will reveal why ethics belongs very much to philosophy and why only philosophy, and not science, psychology or even Smarties, has anything even vaguely approaching the answers when it comes to ethical questions.

Very basically, philosophy is concerned with three main questions, questions that were posed by Plato, the father of Western philosophy, in the far-off days of ancient Greece. In 1929 Alfred North Whitehead famously said that philosophy is 'a series of footnotes to Plato' (*Process and Reality*, p. 39). This is true to the extent that philosophers have spent centuries pondering Plato's key questions and developing various answers.

Plato's key questions are: 'What is there?', 'How do we know what there is?' and 'How should we live given what we know about what there is?' These three questions correspond to the three main branches of philosophy: i) ontology or metaphysics (philosophy of existence), ii) epistemology or theory of knowledge (philosophy of knowing and believing) and last, but by no means least, iii) ethics or morality (philosophy of right conduct).

All the great philosophers are ultimately interested in ethics. Answering ethical questions is the ultimate goal of all their philosophising. This is certainly true of Socrates, Plato, Aristotle, Aquinas, Spinoza, Hume, Rousseau, Kant, Kierkegaard, Nietzsche, Wittgenstein, Sartre and de Beauvoir, to name but a few. They seek to answer ontological and epistemological questions about what there really is and how we know it, in order to answer moral questions about how we should live given what we know about what there is.

If the great philosophers were not interested in ethics they would not deserve to be called great philosophers. Their philosophical vision would be seriously lacking, they would belong only to the countless ranks of logic-chopping academics, small-minded pedants who dabble with philosophy as though it was a chess problem to be solved, a series of abstract technicalities with little bearing on real life and real people.

Great philosophers seek to reveal important truths about how the world really is so that people might be encouraged to be more realistic, to live more in accordance with reality. Great philosophers have a lot to offer people by way of life guidance and advice, even if many of them failed to follow their own advice. That someone does not practise what they preach does not necessarily render their sermon nonsense. Hypocrisy is not necessarily a barrier to truth-telling.

Although great philosophers tend to think alike to a surprising extent, they do not, of course, always agree with one other. Their different interpretations of reality lead them to draw different conclusions about what is the best, wisest and most moral response to reality. Some even reach the nihilistic conclusion that there is no better path, no right or wrong, no meaning to our actions, and certainly not a moral one.

Quite a few great philosophers have been tempted down the nihilistic road to a lesser or greater extent. Some have explored the nihilistic road a considerable distance into the darkness before turning back, before withdrawing from staring too long into the abyss lest the abyss stare into them. 'When you gaze long into an abyss the abyss also gazes into you' (Friedrich Nietzsche, *Beyond Good and Evil*, Aphorism 146, p. 102). Nietzsche, actually, was not a nihilist. Rather, he overcame the 'God is dead' nihilism of his great influence, Arthur Schopenhauer, to show how life might be made meaningful and worthwhile without God, but that is another story.

So, philosophers worth their salt tend towards ethical considerations. Ethics is the icing on the philosophical cake without which the cake is seriously lacking in taste and probably not worth eating. Or perhaps a better cake metaphor is that without ethics the cake is underdone and not fully risen.

Although not all philosophical questions are ethical questions, all truly ethical questions are philosophical questions. Questions about moral values cannot really be answered by science or any other practical discipline. Science can deal with a practical question like, 'Is Donald Trump a natural blond?', but it cannot really deal with a moral question like, 'Is Donald Trump good?' A scientist can investigate what Donald Trump does and maybe even look into why he does it, but a philosopher would still be needed to explain *why* Trump's behaviour is or is not morally good. Although, as I keep saying, there are some philosophers who think that such an explanation is impossible because all moral statements are meaningless.

These philosophers think that it is not possible for Trump, or anyone else for that matter, to be either good or bad. Trump, they argue, is simply a person who some people have positive feelings towards and approve of, and other people have negative feelings towards and disapprove of. Both groups insist they occupy that much sought after location, the moral high ground, when actually there may be no moral high, middle or low ground to occupy. Whether or not there is any real moral ground to be found anywhere is hopefully something you will be better placed to decide for yourself by the end of this philosophical quest in search of that ground.

2
ACHIEVING GOODNESS

Primarily, this chapter looks in detail at the main *moral theories* in philosophy, various ingenious theories that each in their own way attempt to formulate general principles for deciding what goodness is. General principles for distinguishing good from bad, right from wrong, virtue from vice, niceness from naughtiness, righteous conduct from wicked conduct. In formulating general principles for deciding what goodness is, these theories all *prescribe* that we should behave in certain ways if we want to achieve various states that they equate with goodness: rationality, happiness, *eudaimonia* (human flourishing), freedom, authenticity and so on.

Firstly, however, we must chew over, with the aim of spitting them out, a couple of niggling difficulties that appear to deny the very possibility of achieving goodness. Namely, *causal determinism* and *psychological egoism*.

Goodness and Determinism

If a four-year-old child, with no clear understanding of real guns and the havoc they are capable of wreaking, picks up a real, loaded pistol thinking it is a toy, pulls the trigger and blows his mother's brains out, we do not say the child has done a morally bad thing, we do not hold him *morally responsible*. The child did the deed but is not to blame for it, as he was too young and inexperienced to know what he was doing. The killing is not his fault. If anyone is to blame it is the person, perhaps the deceased mother herself, who irresponsibly left a loaded firearm within reach of a young child.

Similarly, an adult with severe learning difficulties who did the same thing would not be held responsible for his actions either, if it was established beyond reasonable doubt that he did not understand, and was not capable of understanding, the broader context of what he was doing, that he was childlike in his reasoning and his limited experience of the world.

Suppose now that an adult of sound mind picked up the gun and, genuinely thinking it was a toy, fired it at his mother for a joke. We would allow that his action was not as reprehensible as that of a person who deliberately shot his mother in cold blood intending to kill her, but we would think of him as responsible for his irresponsible action and therefore worthy of some level of censure if not actual punishment. We would certainly revile him for his stupidity and carelessness, arguing that he ought to have acted with more care given that he was quite capable of doing so.

Suppose he was drunk or high on drugs. Is intoxication a *mitigating* factor? Some argue that it is, and certainly in some cases the law allows intoxication as grounds for reduced liability and therefore reduced punishment. Others argue that a person is responsible for what they do while drunk or high because they were responsible for getting drunk or high. The person should have foreseen that their intoxication would lead to a loss of self-control, and they are therefore responsible for that loss of self-control.

The position taken by a society through its legal system towards a person who commits a crime while intoxicated will often depend on the general attitude of that society towards intoxication. A society that is particularly disapproving of recreational narcotics, for example, may well identify the fact that a person committed a crime while high on one or more such substances as an *aggravating* factor.

We could go on endlessly generating scenarios and deciding on the level of guilt, responsibility and liability involved. Most philosophers and lawyers hold that 'Circumstances alter cases', and certainly much of the highly paid activity of the legal profession is aimed at deciding the level of responsibility in individual cases, the

extent to which a person knew what they w
known what they were doing, could have av
did and so on and so forth.

Were they severely coerced into doing wha.
rob the bank or we will kill your kidnapped family – or was it th.
of coercion that they could easily have resisted had they seriously
wanted to – help us rob the bank or we will cross you off our Christmas
card list?

A court of law seeks to establish, above all, whether or not a
defendant has a *guilty mind*, a *mens rea*. Did the defendant act with
criminal intent, knowing what he was doing, and perceiving and willing
the consequences of what he was doing, or were responsibility and
culpability somehow diminished or entirely lacking? '*Actus reus non
facit reum nisi mens sit rea*,' says the law. 'The act is not culpable
unless the mind is guilty.'

All this, except the Latin, is pretty familiar stuff. Most of us have
watched and read crime and courtroom dramas or know someone
who has ended up in court, even if we have never ended up in court
ourselves. We begin to learn the basic rules of guilt and innocence
from an early age, with parents, siblings, friends, neighbours and
teachers constantly pronouncing on the culpability or otherwise of our
actions. In the vast majority of cases, establishing that someone is or
is not responsible for something, even the extent to which they are
responsible, is not rocket science.

Once all the relevant facts are known deciding whether or not
someone is guilty is more often than not a matter of common sense.
We are even quite well practised at judging the extent to which
particular circumstances alter a case, at recognizing the importance of
mitigating or aggravating factors. If, for example, a woman kills her
husband after he has subjected her to years of physical and mental
abuse, then we easily recognize that extreme *provocation* or even
self-defence come into play, rendering her deed less morally wrong,
not morally wrong at all, or even, as some might argue, a morally
commendable delivery of long overdue justice.

other hand, we think of Ian Stewart, a thoroughly callous calculating man who plied his charming fiancée, the writer Helen Bailey, with sleeping tablets to the point of stupefaction before killing her and her dachshund, Boris, and dumping their remains in a cesspit under their garage, all to get his grasping hands on her money, money she was sharing with him anyway, as particularly abhorrent and culpable and deserving of the full penalty of law. The law agreed and jailed him for thirty-four years.

In judging responsibility in the everyday world we readily presuppose that the phenomenon of moral responsibility exists and that people are undoubtedly morally responsible for their actions in certain familiar and well defined circumstances. Indeed, the human world functions on the basis of a firm belief in the existence of moral responsibility and would perhaps struggle to function without that belief.

But what if no one is ever actually responsible for anything, because every human action is as caused and unavoidable as an ordinary glass window breaking when a house brick strikes it?

The belief that we cannot help doing whatever we do, that all our behaviour is strictly a matter of *cause and effect*, that there is no genuine choice between alternative courses of action, any of which *could* have been chosen before one was chosen, is called *causal determinism*. If all human actions are caused within a wholly deterministic universe then the possibility of genuine moral or immoral behaviour, of genuine goodness or badness, is ruled out.

> If a man could not have done otherwise than he in fact did then he is not responsible for his actions. But if determinism is true, it is true of every action that the agent could not have done otherwise. Therefore, if determinism is true, no one is ever responsible for what he does.
>
> WINSTON NESBITT and STUART CANDLISH,
> 'Determinism and the Ability to do Otherwise', p. 415

So, there can only be genuine goodness and badness where there is genuine moral responsibility, and there can only be genuine moral responsibility where there is genuine *free will*. It seems that before we can explore *how* people might achieve goodness, we have to show that it is *possible* for them to achieve it at all by refuting causal determinism and demonstrating that free will exists.

Well, the way forward is not quite so straightforward because it is impossible to entirely refute causal determinism. Also, free will is a somewhat different animal from the one it is often thought to be at the outset of this particular philosophical investigation.

Causal determinism cannot be entirely refuted but neither can it be proven to be the case. As J. L. Mackie says, 'We do not know whether causal determinism holds or not, in particular whether it holds for all or most human actions' (*Ethics: Inventing Right and Wrong*, p. 215). The problem of causal determinism is rather like the problem of *solipsism*, the view that nothing exists outside the mind and that the external world is an illusion.

Solipsism cannot be utterly refuted, yet, on the other hand, there is no final clinching argument for accepting that it is the case. More importantly perhaps, at the level of ordinary everyday experience, solipsism simply does not appear to be the case. Nobody but a madman or a philosopher goes about their everyday life consistently thinking that the external world does not exist.

Indeed, it is not at all clear what it would be like to behave as a consistent solipsist. A person might argue in the abstract that the external world does not exist, and yet they would find it very difficult if not impossible to behave as though they seriously thought it was not out there. Their behaviour, their daily round, would confirm that they actually thought it was out there.

It is a similar situation with causal determinism. It is impossible to entirely reject on a philosophical level, and yet at the level of ordinary everyday experience it simply does not appear to be the case. We consistently feel that our choices are genuine. That when we choose coffee rather than tea, we *could* have chosen tea. Maybe, just maybe, our choices are not genuine, yet we are never going to start consistently behaving as though they are not genuine. As with behaving like a solipsist, it is not at all clear what would be involved in behaving like a causal determinist.

It is this kind of common-sense approach that one night in 1769 prompted the eminently sensible Dr Samuel Johnson to cut through the Gordian Knot of the free will versus determinism debate during a now famous conversation with his friend and biographer James Boswell. As Boswell recounts: 'Dr. Johnson shunned to-night any discussion of the perplexed question of fate and free will, which I attempted to agitate. "Sir (said he), we *know* our will is free, and *there's* an end on't"' (*Life of Johnson*, p. 411). Johnson was undoubtedly being rather dismissive of what is certainly a 'perplexed question' within the ivory towers of philosophy, but then do we criticize scientists for not troubling to prove the external world is out there before they push on with the far more useful task of researching how the (apparent) external world works?

Worthy though the above common-sense defences of free will are, I have, of course, not yet offered any proper philosophical arguments against the spectre of causal determinism, enough to push it back into its lair and reveal the notions of genuine choice and genuine responsibility as, at the very least, tenable. Time to make amends, then; time to undertake the task of taming causal determinism.

Firstly, is it actually true, as was claimed a while ago, that a man is not responsible for his actions if he could not have done otherwise than he in fact did? Although it might seem blindingly obvious that he is not responsible, there are in fact, at the very least, certain circumstances in which a person who could not have done otherwise *is* nonetheless responsible for his actions.

For example, if you are in a room that, unbeknown to you, is locked, so that you cannot do otherwise than stay in the room, it does not follow that you are not responsible for staying in the room. You may be staying in the room entirely of your own volition, lying on the sofa watching TV with no thought or intention of going out of the room.

For more examples along these lines see Harry G. Frankfurt, 'Alternative Possibilities and Moral Responsibility', pp. 829–39. Sorting out the hornets' nest of philosophical complexities stirred up by this and similar examples is beyond the scope of this book, but clearly the notion of 'could not have done otherwise' is nowhere near as straightforward as it first appeared.

Moving on, it can be said that although many scientifically minded people like to think that the entire universe is governed by causal determinism, it is not at all clear that it is. Quantum theory, the current fundamental theory in physics, is actually *indeterministic*, granting a huge role in the shaping of the universe to probability and even randomness, as opposed to mechanistic inevitability.

In his influential book *The Concept of Mind* (1949) the English philosopher Gilbert Ryle argues that causal determinism arises as a cosmological hypothesis when deterministic mechanical laws that are perfectly appropriate in their proper context – such as the context of a bicycle or car – are misapplied *universally* in an attempt to explain the universe as a whole. As he says:

> People still tend to treat laws of Mechanics not merely as the ideal type of scientific law, but as, in some sense, the ultimate laws of Nature. They tend to hope or fear that biological, psychological and sociological laws will one day be 'reduced' to mechanical laws – though it is left unclear what sort of a transaction the 'reduction' would be.

The Concept of Mind, p. 74

For Ryle, the terms 'determinism' and 'Mechanism' ('Mechanism' as in 'the concept of Mechanism' rather than 'the mechanism') are more or less interchangeable, and he often speaks of the 'bogy of Mechanism' (*The Concept of Mind*, p. 74) where others speak of the bogy or spectre of determinism.

Arguably, the bogy of mechanism/determinism arises, not least, out of a false view of the nature of the scientific process. Contrary to popular belief, it is logically impossible for science to discover *universal laws of nature* that strictly determine the behaviour of the cosmos and everything in it. Science is an inductive process that can do no more than *predict* the future on the basis of past experience. It can only ever establish probabilities, not discover ultimate deterministic principles.

Even if the universe is in a certain sense constrained, not by empirical, causal laws but by the so called laws or rules of logic and mathematics, this still does not imply that it is a machine and us machines along with it. As Ryle points out (*The Concept of Mind*, pp. 74–6), plenty of processes are conducted in accordance with strict rules without the outcome of the process being determined *by* the rules. The rules of football, for example, do not dictate the result of a game of football.

In arguing against Mechanism, Ryle considers the game of chess (*The Concept of Mind*, pp. 74–6). He supposes that what he calls a 'scientifically trained spectator', unacquainted with chess, is 'permitted to look at a chessboard in the intervals between the moves' (*The Concept of Mind*, p. 74). By this process he learns all the rules of chess. When he has done so he is permitted to see that the moves are made by people known as *players*.

According to Ryle, he will take the view that every move the players make in what they believe to be a game of skill is actually 'remorselessly pre-ordained' (*The Concept of Mind*, p. 75) by the rules. Even though he will admit that he cannot yet explain every move by the rules so far discovered, he will assume that further rules exist to explain these moves because it is 'unscientific to suppose that there are inexplicable moves' (*The Concept of Mind*, p. 75).

Aware that a bishop must always move diagonally, for example, he will assume that there are rules dictating the exact number of squares a bishop must move on each occasion. Making Ryle's point, the players will argue against the scientifically trained spectator and insist that 'though every move is governed, not one of them is ordained by the rules' (*The Concept of Mind*, p. 75).

Certainly, if a bishop is moved it will end up on a square of the same colour as that from which it started, but there is no rule stating that it must be moved or how far it is to be moved. As Ryle says, 'There is plenty of room for us to display cleverness and stupidity and to exercise deliberation and choice. Though nothing happens that is irregular, plenty happens that is surprising, ingenious and silly' (*The Concept of Mind*, p. 75).

The players will go on to add that there are, of course, explanations for particular moves made within the rules, though they are not explanations in terms of the rules, but rather in terms of tactical principles. For example, the bishop was moved three squares in order to threaten the opponent's king.

The scientifically trained spectator might reply that tactical principles determine the moves to be made, but this is to forget that there is, except when one is 'backed into a corner' and just about to lose, plenty of scope for alternative tactics, including bad tactics. As Ryle says, 'Knowing how to apply tactical principles involves knowing the rules of the game, but there is no question of these principles being "reducible" to rules of the game' (*The Concept of Mind*, p. 76).

Tactical principles, which make sense in terms of the overall aim of winning, suggest moves, sometimes very strongly, but they do not dictate moves. That a player is motivated to win does not mean that his behaviour is causally determined by *things* called *motives*. As Thomas Reid points out, a motive is not an efficient cause; it is neither an object nor a force. Rather, it has a conceptual reality. A motive, he says, 'May be compared to advice, or exhortation, which leaves a man still at liberty' (*Works of Thomas Reid*, pp. 608–9). Like advice, a motive has no causal efficacy.

Ryle's chess example illustrates that causal determinism has no place in the explanation of certain phenomena. Although chess is heavily rule bound, the outcome of a game of chess is not mechanically dictated by the rules. A game of chess allows for choice, deliberation, responsibility and irresponsibility. In a similar way, though human behaviour is influenced and shaped by desires, fears, motives, reasons, deliberations and so on, these things do not generally dictate our behaviour mechanistically, as the turning of a bicycle wheel is mechanistically dictated by its fixedness within the mechanical system known as a bicycle.

In its particular set-up, the bicycle wheel has no choice. It is free, if not impeded, only to turn. Note that when applied to a determined mechanical event occurring within a particular mechanical system, it even becomes appropriate to speak of x mechanical event taking place *freely*. For a bicycle wheel, to be free is not for it to have free will but for it to perform according to its proper disposition subject to a certain impulsion and free from constraint. This form of freedom is called *liberty of spontaneity*.

In our particular, human psycho-physiological set-up of desires, fears, motives, reasons and deliberations, there is, it seems, scope for genuine choice, for choosing between alternative courses of action, scope for exercising what is called *liberty of indifference*.

It is a common mistake when thinking about free will and choice to suppose that an action is only free when it is determined by nothing, but in truth free will is action in accordance with certain non-mechanistic determinants. An action without determinants of any kind is not actually free but merely random. The key point is that free will and a certain level of determinism are *compatible*. The philosophical position that the two are compatible is called, not surprisingly, *compatibilism*, or sometimes, *soft determinism*, so called to distinguish it from the *hard determinism* of causal determinism.

To insist that free will and determinism are utterly *incompatible* is to insist either that there is no such thing as free will at all, or that free will is simply the complete lack of any determining factors. It is to insist that because free will cannot be determined in any way whatsoever and remain free will, only random, unpredictable, chaotic behaviour can count as an expression of free will.

But to act freely, as opposed to acting in an irrational, incoherent, random manner, requires that the world be predictable to some degree, that there be a coherent framework of needs, desires, motives, objectives and so on within which deliberate, premeditated choices can be made and purposeful, owned courses of action pursued.

If utter chaos reigned and there was no way of establishing hypothetical imperatives of the form 'If you want x then do y', then meaningful action would be impossible and, hence, the possibility of acting freely with any degree of responsibility, moral or otherwise. Just as, outside of a framework of rules, it would be impossible to play a game of chess or freewheel along a freeway.

The only possibility would be to act like the proverbial headless chicken, running about in all directions with no intentions and no responsibility for where it runs. Freedom is not free fall, and to act freely, to be responsible, requires that one act within a situation that has a degree of coherence.

In his major work *Being and Nothingness* (1943) the existentialist philosopher Jean-Paul Sartre does not make a case for free will by attacking determinism; rather, he seeks to show that free will belongs to the very nature of human consciousness to the extent that consciousness simply cannot exist unless it is free.

For Sartre, consciousness is a paradoxical, ambiguous and indeterminate phenomenon that is never at one with itself, never identical with itself. Rather than being a thing in its own right, like a chair, consciousness is nothing but a *relationship* to the world it is consciousness of. Consciousness is nothing in itself, nothing in the present. Consciousness, indeed, is never in the present. It exists only as a perpetual temporal flight or *transcendence* away from the past towards the future. Importantly, as a temporal transcendence towards the future, consciousness stands outside the causal order, the world of cause and effect events.

Events, which are what they are and can never be other than what they are once they have happened, belong to the past, a past that really only exists for a consciousness that is the future of that past. The past exists only for a consciousness that transcends it towards the future. Consciousness exists only as a transcendence of the past towards the future. Consciousness is the future of the past, which is to say it is the future *possibilities* of the past. As nothing but a being towards the future, as nothing but the future possibilities of what it transcends, consciousness has to be those possibilities. It cannot not be an opening up of possibilities.

Sartre's key point about free will is that we are able to be free in a world of mechanical cause and effect events because we constantly escape that mechanical world towards the future. It is in the future at which we aim that we are free.

The freedom of consciousness consists in the perpetual opening up of the possibilities of situations. Consciousness discovers itself in a world of possibilities that it creates because it is a perpetual *futurizing intention*. Consciousness is not *in* the future; the future exists only as the 'not yet' towards which consciousness flees. Furthermore, the future can never be reached because to 'reach' the future is to immediately render it past. Nonetheless, it is in the future at which consciousness aims that consciousness is free, free in the sense of having a range of future possibilities which it realizes for itself.

By choosing among its possibilities, by choosing a course of action, consciousness brings some of its possibilities into actuality and abandons others. The transformation of possibility into actuality is the transformation of what existentialist philosophers call *future-past* into *past-future*. The past is a past-future, a one-time future that has now passed into the past. Some of the possibilities that comprise consciousness get transformed into a past-future and this past-future immediately becomes the launch pad for a further transcendence by consciousness towards new future possibilities.

The fact that consciousness has to be a futurizing intention in order to exist at all, the fact that it cannot not be an opening-up of possibilities, implies that it cannot not be free. For Sartre, to be free is to have to constantly make choices, including moral choices, choices for which the person making them is responsible.

This unending responsibility is such a burden to some people that they *choose* to behave as though they are not free, to act as though they inhabit a deterministic universe where choice is impossible and events simply act upon them. Sartre calls this ongoing disingenuous attempt to live as though one were not free, this dodging of responsibility, *bad faith*. Bad faith is displayed, for example, by people who insist they are not responsible for their role in a massacre or some other atrocity because they were 'only following orders'. Such is 'the banality of evil' on many occasions.

As Arendt points out in *Eichmann in Jerusalem: A Report on the Banality of Evil*, as an officer in the SS, Otto Eichmann played a significant role in perpetrating the Holocaust. At his trial, however, he flatly denied, absolutely and impassively, *any* responsibility, insisting on the *superior orders* or *Nuremberg defence*. He refused to recognize that *existentially* to follow orders is to *choose* to follow orders. The absurd implication of the Nuremberg defence is that Adolf Hitler *alone* was at fault for the atrocities of the entire Third Reich. More on existentialist ethics later in this chapter.

There is a lot more that could be said on the free will and determinism debate, but as I cannot go into a book-length digression here, I shall move swiftly on in the hope that at the very least I have shown that it is by no means proven that causal determinism undermines the possibility of moral responsibility. Hopefully, I have shown that genuine moral responsibility, especially if we understand the nature of determinism, consciousness, free will and responsibility correctly, is at least as plausible a notion as the existence of the external world.

Scientists get on fine analysing the external world without proving beyond all doubt that it exists. We will get on fine analysing goodness without proving beyond all doubt that universal causal determinism is not the case. There is no convincing evidence that universal causal determinism is the case, just as there is no convincing evidence that solipsism is the case, and it is certainly not insignificant that both are entirely counter-intuitive.

Goodness and Egoism

There is a second difficulty that appears on the face of it to deny the very possibility of achieving goodness, namely *psychological egoism*. Psychological egoism is a familiar notion. Its advocates, Thomas Hobbes in his book *Leviathan* (1651), for example, claim that it is a fact or law of human nature that we cannot act other than in our own self-interest, that however the case may appear, there is no such thing as an unselfish motive.

For sure, people often do good deeds at least partly for their own self-interest. I help my neighbour lay his slabs partly because I want him to think well of me, partly because I hope he will help me with my tasks in future, and partly because I get healthy exercise and pleasure from getting stuck into a building job, especially one I can wash my hands of when I want. But perhaps I also help him because I like him or because I feel it is my moral duty to help others or because I am a social animal unthinkingly driven by an instinct for cooperation.

Also, we all know virtue-signalling goody-goodies, or see them on television. People who are so busy doing good deeds, so full of barely concealed smugness that they are single-handedly saving the world, that it is pretty obvious to anyone with an ounce of scepticism that they are significantly motivated by feeling good about *themselves* and being holier than thou. Like Mrs Jellyby in Charles Dickens's *Bleak House* (1853), they often neglect their own nearest and dearest in favour of the greater personal reward of helping humankind as a whole, a group best represented by far-away strangers.

But the advocates of psychological egoism insist that all people everywhere are for all time unavoidably determined by base human nature only and ever to do so-called good deeds for their own self-interest, that it is impossible for them to do otherwise than seek to advance their own cause in everything they do. So-called philanthropists undoubtedly benefit many others by their so-called philanthropy, but doing so is not and cannot be their real or ultimate goal. The theory of psychological egoism holds that goodness is never more than a mere facade. Scratch the surface of this thin veneer and all you will find is selfishness and egotism.

Such, for example, is the harsh teaching of Thomas Gradgrind in Dickens's *Hard Times* (1854), who eventually has the principle of psychological egoism flung against his personal concerns for his delinquent son by his coldly logical star pupil, Bitzer:

'I beg your pardon for interrupting you, sir,' returned Bitzer; 'but I am sure you know that the whole social system is a question of self-interest. What you must always appeal to, is a person's self-interest. It's your only hold. We are so constituted. I was brought up in that catechism when I was very young, sir, as you are aware.'

Hard Times, p. 277

This is not to say that people always succeed in advancing their own selfish ends. They may be mistaken as to the means to the selfish ends they wish to achieve and may even inadvertently end up benefiting others more than themselves, but nonetheless benefiting others more than themselves was not and cannot be their real aim.

Psychological egoism is a superficially neat and simple reductionist theory. It reduces the apparent complexities of human behaviour, interaction and motivation to a minimal principle. This very simplicity makes it appealing to those who, like Gradgrind, pretend to great wisdom on the basis of a hackneyed, one-size-fits-all interpretation of human nature. It also appeals to cynics, scrooges, grumps and grouches everywhere because it justifies their personal meanness and misanthropy. Certainly, psychological egoism, like many theories in philosophy and science, is far easier to outline than refute. Nonetheless, it can be refuted. It can be shown to be simple, not in the sense of *elegant*, but in the sense of *simplistic*.

Just because it is possible to *interpret* everything that people do in terms of psychological egoism does not mean that it is correct to do so. We have to ask, where is the *empirical evidence* that psychological egoism is the case? For sure, there are those goody-goody people we mentioned earlier who do good deeds primarily to feel good about themselves, but remember that the theory of psychological egoism maintains that all people only and ever act in their own self-interest.

No sufficiently thorough empirical investigation of human motives has been conducted, or seemingly could ever be conducted, that would prove psychological egoism to be the case. Not least, human motives are not always transparent, and even our own motives are often opaque to ourselves. Yet the advocates of psychological egoism claim to know for certain that selfishness is always the real motive for every action, even when the evidence seems to suggest otherwise.

Martyrdom, for example, is always celebrated as the ultimate selfless act and appears to involve no self-interest. Surely, there can be nothing selfish in sacrificing one's life to a cause, as one has surrendered everything and gained nothing that one can personally enjoy.

Not surprisingly, advocates of psychological egoism reply that when any case of so called selflessness is examined more closely, it is inevitably revealed as a case of selfishness. They argue, for example, that a mother's true motivation in nursing her sick child is her own peace of mind. As to martyrs, even the voluntary martyr is acting in his own self-interest because he is seeking glory or a stairway to heaven.

This is certainly true of *some* so-called martyrs. Suicide bombers, for example, who are as selfish as they are stupid, blowing themselves and as many innocent civilians as they can to smithereens in the misguided belief that God will reward them with countless willing virgins in an eternal paradise. But what about the atheist soldier who, though he would like to go on living, volunteers to fight and die to save his homeland? Is he selfish?

Aware of the endless problems inherent in investigating motives themselves, advocates of psychological egoism argue that psychological egoism is a necessary truth grounded in a conceptual analysis of human *action*. In the case of helping others, their argument runs something like this:

Jane wants to help John.

If Jane is doing what she wants then she is satisfying a desire.

If Jane is satisfying a desire then she is removing a frustration.

To remove or seek to remove frustrations is to act egoistically.

Therefore, Jane is acting egoistically.

This argument appears to be sound but actually it is equivocal, if not damned right slippery, in its use of 'wants'. Crucially, must the fact that Jane *wants* to help John be reduced to another want? Namely, the wanting to satisfy a desire and remove a frustration? Advocates of psychological egoism introduce a needless or bogus second-level want. They assume that all apparently other-directed, altruistic wants must be reduced to a self-directed, egoistic want. Rather than simply accept that Jane wants to help John, they insist that what Jane *really* wants is her wanting to help John to be satisfied, as in, 'I want to help John *because* I want my desire to help him to be satisfied.'

But why introduce a second-level, self-directed want to account for the first? Why can't we make sense of wanting to help another person in terms that do not reduce that want to another want? Why shouldn't the first-level want be sufficient? If the first-level want is not sufficient, we tend towards an infinite regress of wants, where every want is only 'explicable' in terms of a deeper, more basic, more egocentric want.

So, the simple theory of psychological egoism actually ends up over-complicating any analysis of human action by introducing confusing and unnecessary levels of want and desire into the picture. As said, psychological egoism is simplistic in its simplicity, not elegant. Psychological egoism descends into reducing wants to other wants, when the simple, sensible, productive way forward is actually to consider what it is about helping others that makes most people want to do it.

The strongest argument against psychological egoism is that we can only gain pleasure from helping others if there is something of genuine, intrinsic value in helping others, quite apart from the pleasure we get from doing it. If, for example, the mother did not genuinely care for her sick child, if she was not able to value anything other than her own self-interest, she would gain no satisfaction from nursing the poor little mite back to health. Unless she genuinely loved the child, its recovery would give her no pleasure.

Surely, her maternal love alone is sufficient to cause the mother to act. The result of doing the act should not be confused with the reason or purpose which prompted the mother to act in the first place. Just because the mother gets satisfaction from doing something, it does not follow that she did it purely *for the sake of* enjoying that satisfaction, particularly when there would not be any satisfaction unless she wanted to do the thing anyway. If we do not, indeed cannot, genuinely care for others, as the advocates of psychological egoism suggest, then surely we would gain no satisfaction from helping them.

So, psychological egoism does not stack up as a theory, and certainly, as with causal determinism, there is no argument available capable of convincing us that it is the case. As a result, altruism, that key ingredient of goodness, is spared the insult of being dismissed as impossible.

Psychological egoism and the unselfish concern for the welfare of others we call *altruism* are entirely incompatible, because the former, if true, would leave no room for the latter. This is not to say, however, that egoism and altruism are never compatible, for there is a form of egoism that sits perfectly well with altruism, namely *rational egoism*.

Unlike advocates of psychological egoism, advocates of rational egoism do not claim that egoism is a *law* of psychology, that we are psychologically *hardwired* to be completely selfish. Unlike the theory of psychological egoism, which insists that we are *determined* by our nature always to act in accordance with what we perceive to be our own self-interest, the theory of rational egoism allows that we are *free* to behave rationally or irrationally.

Advocates of rational egoism argue that egoism is a *criterion of rational behaviour*, that it is rational to act in our own self-interest and that a person who does not have a pattern of conduct that *tends* to benefit him is a fool. Rational egoism does not claim, as psychological egoism does, that there cannot be genuine altruism, but it does insist that there are *reasonable limits* to altruism, that a certain level of selfishness is both judicious and moral.

In his *Sermons* (1726) the English bishop, theologian and philosopher Joseph Butler attacks the psychological egoism of Hobbes. Butler nonetheless advocates *self-love*. Not Hobbesian *hot self-love*, but rather Butlerian *cool self-love*, a moderate degree of self-love, which he argues is both rational and ethical. It is often argued in ethics that what is truly rational is also ethical, a theme we will explore further when we come to examine Kant's moral theory.

Examining rational egoism reveals more clearly what altruism really is, reveals that it need not be a complete lack of egoism and self-interest. Indeed, it may well be the case that altruism requires a degree of self-interest in order to function effectively. For instance, an excessively altruistic man who gives all his resources to the poor is likely to become an impoverished charity case himself, a man unable any longer to behave altruistically.

The moral theory of Aristotle, which we will consider in detail in due course, recommends moderation and balance in all things. The excessively altruistic, excessively generous man is not virtuous; in fact he commits the vice of wastefulness and profligacy. What constitutes reasonable generosity and altruism for an individual depends on his particular wealth and circumstances.

In allowing that we have free will, rational egoism is able to take into account cases where people are completely selfless. It remains a matter of debate, however, whether a completely selfless act, in lacking cool self-love, can be considered moral if it cannot be considered rational. The completely selfless act is often considered to be the height of virtue, but is it really so? As with so much in ethics, the answer we give seems to depend upon the particular case in question.

Arguably, a man who cannot swim who dives into a lake to save another man from drowning is not acting morally but foolishly. Presumably, if he cannot swim he will not save the drowning man and will drown himself. Yet we *can* make sense of the notion of it being both moral and rational to die for another, particularly in cases where the other gains some definite advantage that the martyr wished them to have. Overall, the problem seems to lie in the impossibility of establishing strict rules for what is and is not rational. Some cases of irrationality are clear-cut, where a person's actions are plainly stupid. But other cases are far less than clear-cut.

Does a voluntary martyr act irrationally in acting against his own self-interest, or is it sometimes rational to act against one's own self-interest, particularly if some great and lasting good for others results from it? Is it possible to be irrational but moral, rational but immoral? It depends how closely morality and rationality are equated. How closely they are equated, how closely they should be equated, is an issue upon which philosophers differ, although certainly it seems fair to say that the majority of philosophers argue that morality and rationality are equated to some extent.

For their part, existentialist philosophers tend to argue that voluntary martyrdom is not a matter of reason or unreason but simply a matter of personal choice. The voluntary martyr simply *chooses* to die for others and/or for what he believes. He may have had his *own* reasons which perhaps he did not examine too closely, he may have acted on the basis of a *feeling* that this was the right thing to do, he may have acted out of sheer bloody-mindedness. What matters in the end is that he committed himself to an irrevocable action and took the plunge.

Kant argues that being free means acting rationally in accordance with a certain core rational principle. We will explore that principle in due course. For other.thinkers, Sartre for example, being free means having the freedom to attach value to certain actions and not to others. For Sartre, there are no values in the world other than those we choose to create on the basis of our freedom. 'My freedom is the unique foundation of values, and *nothing*, absolutely nothing, justifies my adoption of this or that value, this or that scale of values' (*Being and Nothingness*, p. 62).

For Sydney Carton, the hero of Dickens's *A Tale of Two Cities* (1859), a novel set during the French Revolution, ultimate value attaches to making his death a noble and generous deed, to suffering the guillotine to save the family of the woman he loves. 'It is a far, far better thing that I do, than I have ever done; it is a far, far better rest that I go to, than I have ever known' (*A Tale of Two Cities*, p. 390).

Sydney Carton dying to save the family of the woman he loves might be interpreted as rational, irrational, brave, foolish, selfless, ultimately selfish and so on. Who can settle the question? Not even

Carton himself – even if he was a non-fictional character and his severed head could pass comment from beyond the grave. This suggests that there is no final answer as to what his motives really were. We might want to say that what he did was certainly impressive, even if it was foolish and, in a certain sense, vainglorious. It would be a hard-hearted judge who was not moved to admire Carton's deed, especially given the emotional power of Dickens's narrative, but admiring a deed does not make it moral or rational.

Finally, it is worth adding that it is a short step from rational egoism to *ethical egoism*. Ethical egoism claims that it is morally right for a person to pursue his own good according to his abilities and, perhaps more interestingly, that it is immoral to be *un-egoistic*, for a person to un-egoistically waste his talents and opportunities, for example. Aristotle makes a similar claim in his moral theory.

Advocates of ethical egoism recognize that if it is right for you to pursue your own goals to the limits of your ability, then it is right for others to do so too. It follows, therefore, that you must respect the moral right of others to pursue their goals whilst you are in pursuit of yours and vice versa. Clearly, there must be compromise, and out of this compromise arise familiar, everyday, practical ethical notions such as sharing and waiting your turn.

Theories of Goodness in General

We are rapidly approaching the point where we can begin setting out and examining the main *moral theories*; theories that seek to provide grounds for distinguishing moral goodness from moral badness, right action from wrong action; theories that strive to establish exactly what goodness is and how to achieve it. However, before we look at each of these wonderful theories *individually*, it is worth laying down a few guidelines concerning the nature of moral theories *in general*. These guidelines will undoubtedly stand your understanding in good stead as we move forward.

Some moral philosophers called *deontologists* (*deontology* derives from the Greek *deon*, meaning *obligation* or *duty*) argue that certain human actions are right or wrong in themselves or, more precisely, right or wrong under particular specified *rules* rather than right or wrong according to the *consequences* they produce. Deontology tends to lead to the view that there are fixed moral truths or principles that apply to every person regardless of their circumstances. For Kant and those deontologists who follow him most closely, these unchanging moral truths or principles can be discovered or established through pure reason. For them, ethics is a matter of *a priori* knowledge, that is knowledge gained prior to or apart from empirical, sensory experience.

On the other hand, another group of moral philosophers called *consequentialists* argue that no human action is right or wrong in itself or, more precisely, that no human action is fundamentally or categorically right or wrong. The rightness or wrongness of an action has to be judged empirically, experientially, according to the consequences it produces. Consequentialists disagree with deontologists that ethics is a matter of *a priori* knowledge or pure reasoning. For them, ethics is a common-sense business involving the practical, empirical assessment of the consequences of human actions in the real world.

The split between deontologists and consequentialists, with the former looking to pure reason to decide questions of right and wrong and the latter looking to empirical evidence, is an aspect of the greatest divide in philosophy, the gulf between *rationalists* and *empiricists*; between *rationalism* and *empiricism*. This divide is found in many areas of philosophy. It is the product of a broad, ongoing, centuries-old, heated debate about the true nature and source of knowledge, including moral knowledge.

Although they are on either side of the great divide, both deontologists and consequentialists are, broadly speaking, *moral objectivists*. That is, they believe that there are objective moral facts or, at least, that there are objective means of establishing that an action is right or wrong. They simply disagree about the means.

This sets them apart from various groups of philosophers who are very sceptical that there is any genuine way of *judging* right from wrong. These philosophers, collectively known as *moral subjectivists*, argue that there are no moral truths or principles, that ethical statements are neither true nor false but essentially meaningless. They argue that what appear to be moral assertions laying claim to underlying moral principles, such as 'Giving to charity is good' or 'Stealing is wrong', are really just expressions of feeling and emotion, expressions of approval or disapproval. More on the debate between moral subjectivists and moral objectivists in Chapter 3: 'The Reality of Goodness'.

On the side of moral objectivism, what is called *normative* or *substantive* ethics attempts to formulate general principles for distinguishing good from bad, right from wrong. Normative ethics attempts to find a coherent and defensible basis for ethical principles and values. The term *normative* is a big giveaway here, the definition of *normative* being: establishing, relating to, or deriving from a standard or norm, especially of behaviour.

There are basically three normative moral theories: i) *deontological, duty based or Kantian ethics*; ii) *utilitarianism or consequentialism*; and iii) *virtue or Aristotelian ethics*. We will examine each in turn under the headings: 'Goodness and Duty'; 'Goodness and Happiness'; and 'Goodness and the Golden Mean'. We will also take a look at existentialist ethics, as a moral theory that is somewhat different from the three aforementioned *classic* theories, under the heading 'Goodness and Freedom'. Why? Well, because existentialist ethics is interesting, because it offers a novel angle on the nature of goodness and virtue, and because variety is the spice of life.

I want to say, we are finally ready to proceed, but I trust that we have been *proceeding* steadily since the start of this book, given that clearing the scrub, improving the access, sinking the footings and establishing the guidelines are all essential to the process of building that steel and glass palace as seen on *Grand Designs*.

Goodness and Duty

In philosophical terms, the great German philosopher Immanuel Kant definitely can. Not only did he synthesize the long divided traditions of rationalism and empiricism in his monumental *Critique of Pure Reason* (1781) and other profound works, imposing a new rigour and direction on philosophical thinking, but for an encore he came up with his own moral theory. Deontological or duty-based ethics is largely the brainchild of Kant's enormous brain and as such is often referred to as *Kantian ethics*.

Kant's moral theory is set out in his 1785 masterpiece *Groundwork of the Metaphysic of Morals*. In this short, concise book Kant seeks to establish that reason, rational thinking, is the basis of morality and to reveal that certain actions are *intrinsically* right or wrong, regardless of their consequences.

With his usual crystal-clear sense of direction Kant hits the ground running by arguing, at the very start of his first chapter, that the only thing in the world that is entirely and unconditionally good, good without qualification, is a *good will*. Other talents and qualities of temperament are often good and desirable, such as courage or patience, but they are not good without qualification because when directed by a will that is not good they often prove to be extremely bad, hurtful and damaging.

> It is impossible to conceive of anything at all in the world, or even out of it, which can be taken as good without qualification, except a *good will*. Intelligence, wit, judgement, and any other *talents* of the mind we may care to name, or courage, resolution and constancy of purpose, as qualities of *temperament*, are without doubt good and desirable in many respects; but they can also be extremely bad and hurtful when the will is not good which has to make use of these gifts of nature.
>
> *Groundwork of the Metaphysic of Morals*, p. 59

Patience, for instance, although often a virtue, can be a great vice when directed by a bad will. The patient serial killer, for example, who bides his time, waiting for the ideal opportunity to strike, will be even more deadly than the hasty serial killer who rushes in without thinking. The patient serial killer is less likely to be caught and therefore more likely to prolong his activities. The same can be said for the intelligent or resolute serial killer. Intelligence and resolution are, as Kant points out, good and desirable in many respects, but certainly not when they are among the character traits of a mass murderer.

Kant notes that many people have qualities of character and temperament that can make the task of the good will easier. They are, for example, naturally moderate in their affections or given to sober reflection. These are often good qualities to have, and 'may even seem to constitute part of the *inner* worth of a person' (*Groundwork*, p. 60). But they are not *unconditionally* good, as once again they can prove to be very bad qualities when driven by a bad will. In Kant's view, therefore, such qualities of character and temperament should not be overly esteemed, as he believes they are by the ancients, Aristotle in particular.

Philosophers offer a range of services and they are certainly in the business of exposing the blindingly obvious, exposing what is so obvious it is easily overlooked. It was obvious once you found your keys that they were in the lock, yet you wasted ten minutes of your precious time searching for them. Stating the obvious, or perhaps the not so obvious before it is stated, Kant points out that the goodness of a good will consists entirely in its *willing good*. Actually, his purpose in stating the obvious here is to lead neatly into his next point, which is that the goodness of a good will does not lie in what its good intentions *achieve* but only in the fact that it wills good.

Kant, as said, is a deontologist not a consequentialist; he does not believe that the moral goodness of actions is to be judged in any way by their consequences. For him, what makes actions good or bad is that they are or are not driven by a *good will*.

There is a tendency among commentators on Kant's ethics to say that for Kant actions are inherently good or bad, good or bad in themselves. Although this perhaps serves as a first approximation towards understanding Kant's position, serves to differentiate it from the view that actions are not good or bad in themselves but good or bad according to their consequences, it must always be remembered that for Kant it is the *will* behind the action that makes it good or bad.

Having a good will is not simply *feeling* that your heart is in the right place when you do something. It is not vaguely undertaking to *mean well*. As the proverb says, the road to hell is paved with good intentions. Having a good will is not even having an *inclination* to will good. Having a good will is behaving in strict accordance with a particular, all-important, rational principle that Kant calls the *categorical imperative*. This rational principle lies at the very heart of Kantian ethics; it is the bright sun around which the entire Kantian ethical solar system revolves.

Kant is out to reveal the only way, in his view, that morality is possible, out to give morality a foothold in reality, out to root it in clear, rational action. What he is not out to do is vaguely assume, as most people do, that morality is about inclinations, misguided or otherwise, and fuzzy, often mawkish feelings of compassion and pity. Helping others, for example, out of an inclination to do so is not immoral, except on those occasions where it is somehow in breach of the categorical imperative, but neither is it moral unless it is also behaviour in accordance with the categorical imperative.

As moral behaviour is only behaviour in accordance with the categorical imperative, it is quite possible to behave morally despite having no personal inclination to behave in a certain way. As far as moral behaviour is concerned, inclination and all the rest of it are irrelevant. Basic moral behaviour consists entirely in fulfilling one's duty to the rational principle of the categorical imperative.

In a sense, the clearest example of a truly moral person is a person who does not want to do something but does it anyway because they know it is their moral duty. Or rather, to be more precise, the clearest example of a truly moral person is a person who wants to do something but refrains from doing it because they know doing it would be a breach of their moral duty.

It is sometimes unfairly said that the categorical imperative, and by implication Kant's moral philosophy as a whole, is far more about what you should not do than what you should do, but to say this is to ignore that, for Kant, what you *should do* is act in accordance with the categorical imperative. Appraising actions in terms of the categorical imperative reveals what actions are morally *acceptable* precisely because that appraisal identifies, eliminates and outlaws what actions are morally *unacceptable*.

Kant's moral philosophy is also very much concerned with the distinction between *perfect duties* of justice and *imperfect duties* of humanity and benevolence. Perfect duties are fulfilled by *not doing* something, not stealing for example. Paying a debt is also a perfect duty. Paying a debt is, of course, *doing something*, but from a perfect duty perspective to pay a debt is to *not* violate the categorical imperative and *not* violate a creditor's right to payment.

Perfect duties constitute a moral minimum that is often enforced by law, whereas imperfect duties go beyond that minimum and are not usually enforced by law. It is not *necessary* to fulfil imperfect duties but it is *desirable* and doing so makes a person virtuous, so long as they are also respecting perfect duties that is. Giving to charity is an imperfect duty, it is not compulsory but it is nonetheless a morally good thing to do. Kant argues that perfect duties are determinate, they can only be fulfilled in one way, whereas imperfect duties are indeterminate and can be fulfilled in various ways as a person sees fit. Perfect duties permit no flexibility whereas imperfect duties permit a considerable degree of flexibility.

So, what is this all-important categorical imperative, this mighty Kantian principle upon which so much turns? 'After all this build-up, it better be good,' I hear you say. Well, Kant expresses the principle in various ways in his *Groundwork*, but the most straightforward and well-known formulation is this: 'Act only on that maxim through which you can at the same time will that it should become a universal law' (*Groundwork*, p. 84). 'Is that it?', I hear you cry. 'Is that what all the build-up was about? Not even sure what it means!' Well, for sure, it certainly requires some unpacking to reveal its meaning, to reveal what a philosophically fine and eminently sensible principle it is.

The categorical imperative appears at first sight to involve doing unto others as you would have them do unto you. This is the so-called *golden rule*, as expressed in various places in the Bible. 'So in everything, do to others what you would have them do to you, for this sums up the Law of Moses and the teachings of the prophets' (Matthew 7:12).

The golden rule is undoubtedly a fairly sensible rule of thumb to include in your common-sense ethical toolkit, one that assumes that people the world over want the same pleasant things and only those things: to be free from hunger, homelessness, pain and poverty, to have food, shelter, medicine and money, to be treated with respect, to be helped when in need and so on. As The Human League once said in a song called 'Things That Dreams Are Made Of', making a fair and largely true generalization, everyone requires love, affection, adventure, spending money and a few friends.

Beyond the basics, however, people do not all have exactly the same wants. Some people want to be bound in bondage gear and a gimp mask, hung upside-down from the rafters and whipped, others do not. That some people want others to do this to them does not mean that they have a right to do this to others without their consent. The golden rule soon begins to fail, certainly as a *fundamental* rule of morality, as we inevitably find ourselves needing to bring in other moral concepts, like consent, to prop it up.

Amazingly, in 2001, in Germany, Bernd Jürgen Armando Brandes consented to be eaten by the Rotenburg Cannibal, Armin Meiwes. The two started by attempting to eat Brandes's severed penis, before Meiwes killed Brandes and ate a significant amount of his flesh. That Brandes wanted to be eaten would not, as the golden rule claims, make it ok for him to eat others, any more than it was ok for Meiwes to eat Brandes. Incidentally, Meiwes, originally convicted of manslaughter but later retried and convicted of murder, now claims to regret his actions and has become a vegetarian.

Far from being a glorified version of the golden rule, the categorical imperative involves asking yourself, 'What if everyone did this?', before you go ahead and do whatever it is you are thinking of doing. If it is the sort of thing that would become impossible for anyone to do if everyone tried to do it all the time then it is your moral duty not to do it.

Take false promising, for example – making a promise with no intention of keeping it. A more mundane example than extreme sadomasochism no doubt, but probably one more suited to our calm, philosophical purposes. Kant notes that in considering the consequences of making a false promise, a person may well see the personal advantage of doing so on a particular occasion (*Groundwork*, p. 67). He may, for example, extricate himself from financial embarrassment by borrowing money with no intention of paying it back.

If he is prudent, however, he will see that this is not a wise way to proceed. He will gain a reputation for being untrustworthy and as such may be unable to secure loans in future. 'I do indeed see that it is not enough for me to extricate myself from present embarrassment by this subterfuge: I have to consider whether from this lie there may not subsequently accrue to me much greater inconvenience than that from which I now escape' (*Groundwork*, p. 67). In the end, the *consequences* of borrowing money with no intention of paying it back, and indeed not paying it back, may well be worse than the current financial embarrassment from which he seeks to extricate himself.

However, as Kant points out, whether or not it is prudent to make a false promise has nothing whatsoever to do with whether or not it is morally right to make a false promise. As he says:

To tell the truth for the sake of [moral] duty is something entirely different from doing so out of concern for inconvenient results; for in the first case the concept of the action already contains in itself a law for me, while in the second case I have first of all to look around elsewhere in order to see what effects may be bound up with it for me.

Groundwork, p. 68

A *maxim* is a general principle established by action, and in order to decide whether or not making a false promise is morally right I have only to consider whether or not the maxim of getting out of difficulties by false promising can hold as a *universal law*.

If I decide that I will only make false promises to escape difficulties that I can escape in no other way, then I establish this as a maxim, not only for myself but for everyone. I am, in effect, declaring that everyone can make false promises whenever it suits them to do so. The problem with this, as Kant points out, is that although I can will to lie, 'I can by no means will a universal law of lying; for by such a law there could properly be no promises at all' (*Groundwork*, p. 68).

By such a law, I could never give anyone a promise, as no one would accept my assurances, and no one could ever give me a promise, as I could never accept their assurances. A maxim of false promising cannot hold as a universal law, cannot be willed as a universal law, for as soon as it became a universal law it would unavoidably annul itself by annulling the practice of promising altogether. Hence false promising is immoral.

So, Kant argues that you should only act on maxims that you can will to become a universal law. A maxim of false promising, for example, cannot be willed as a universal law in the way that a maxim of real promising, for example, can be willed as a universal law. It is possible for everyone to tell the truth universally, but it is not possible for everyone to lie universally.

For a person to adopt *non*-universalizable maxims in his treatment of others is for him to treat others as a *means to his own ends*, rather than respect them as *ends in themselves*. If I lie to someone, or give him a false promise, or steal from him, or rape him, or murder him, then I am using him for my own ends and goals rather than respecting him as a free being with his own ends and goals.

In Kant's terms, I am treating him as a *mere* means rather than as an end in himself. Acting in accordance with the categorical imperative when dealing with others, acting only on maxims that can be universalized, ensures that I always respect others as ends in themselves and never exploit them as mere means to my own ends. In writing about what he calls 'the formula of the end in itself' Kant says:

The value of all objects that can *be produced* by our actions is always conditioned. Beings whose existence depends, not on our will, but on nature, have none the less, if they are non-rational beings, only a relative value as means and are consequently called *things*. Rational beings, on the other hand, are called *persons* because their nature already marks them out as ends in themselves – that is, as something which ought not to be used merely as a means – and consequently imposes to that extent a limit on all arbitrary treatment of them (and is an object of reverence). Persons, therefore, are not merely subjective ends whose existence as an object of our actions has a value *for us*: they are *objective ends* – that is, things whose existence is in itself an end, and indeed an end such that in its place we can put no other end to which they should serve *simply* as means.

Groundwork, pp. 90–1

Of course, we all treat each other as a means. I use the taxi driver to get to the shops and he uses me to earn a living, but this arrangement is or should be consensual, both parties having entered into it freely. I have used the taxi driver as a means, but not as a *mere* means. I have not disrespected his freedom and right to self-determination as I would do if I avoided paying for my taxi ride or mugged him at the end of my journey.

For Kant, to act morally is to act logically in accordance with the rational principle of the categorical imperative. Interestingly, only by acting in accordance with this rational principle, this rule, does a person cease to be determined by universal causation; cease to be swept along by his desires like a leaf in a torrent. Only dutiful action in accordance with the categorical imperative allows a person to rise above the causal order of nature and determine his own actions.

Freedom, for Kant, is not doing as you please, but doing what is morally right – that is, acting in accordance with the categorical imperative. Freedom cannot be doing as you please, because to do as you please is to be a slave to your desires. Freedom is rational self-determination.

Kant's moral theory is certainly clear-cut, providing crystal-clear guidance on what constitutes moral goodness. It brilliantly identifies the deeper reasoning behind many of our most familiar and age-old moral rules. 'Thou shalt not kill', 'Thou shalt not steal', 'Thou shalt not bear false witness'. Why? Well, not only because, according to the Bible, God said so, but because to kill, steal or lie is to establish maxims that are in breach of the categorical imperative and therefore treat other rational beings as mere means rather than as ends in themselves.

In establishing an absolute, unqualified moral principle, in rising above cultural norms and practices to the level of universally and unconditionally applicable reason, Kant's moral theory clearly establishes that certain cultural practices – slavery, cannibalism, human sacrifice, the systematic oppression of women within certain patriarchal religions, the exploitation and injustice that thrives within caste systems and so on – are absolutely morally inexcusable and intolerable anywhere at any time.

Advocates of what is called *moral progress* argue that it is possible for people to become more moral over time. Kant's moral theory certainly offers universal, rational moral standards against which the moral progress of people can be measured. The more people and their societies abandon those cultural practices that Kantian ethics exposes as unacceptable, and the more aligned with Kantian duty-based ethics they become, the more moral progress they can be said to have made.

Kant envisages a *kingdom of ends*, a world in which people never use each other as a mere means and always respect each other as free, rational ends in themselves. This, for Kant, would be the ideal moral state. Given the way most people are, or have always been – greedy, selfish, deceitful, weak-willed and so on – it seems this ideal moral state will never be achieved. It is, however, a logically possible distant dream worth aiming for. Something that, in a sense, we aim for every time our other-person-related-actions are in accordance with the prime moral principle of the categorical imperative.

Kant's great successor George Hegel sees history as the progressive development of human reason towards perfect rationality.

Hegel's future perfected state of humankind, achieved through perfecting the institutions that comprise the human world, systems of education, technology, law, politics and so on, would be similar to Kant's kingdom of ends, with everyone always acting perfectly rationally in complete accordance with universal moral principles.

Some critics argue that Kant offers no real *incentive*, at least in this life, to be good. Telling people that only by acting morally will they fulfil their rational duty, and only by fulfilling their rational duty will they be free, hardly seems enough to inspire most people to a life of virtue. People will still *feel* that they have free will regardless of how they behave and that will be sufficient for most of them. Who concerns themselves with such obscurities? Only a very philosophically minded person would live according to the categorical imperative in order to know that doing so made them free.

Against all this it can be argued that Kant is not in the business of *incentivizing* people to be good, he is not a lifestyle guru. He is in the business of explaining what constitutes goodness. Some will aspire to live accordingly, others will remain governed by desire, treating others as a *mere* means to their own selfish ends.

Actually, Kant does incentivize the virtuous by seeking to show them that their virtue will eventually be rewarded with complete happiness, if not in this life then in the hereafter. In his *Critique of Practical Reason*, he argues that the perfect moral state of the *summum bonum* (highest good) is achieved when a person becomes both completely virtuous and completely happy.

For Kant, the *summum bonum* is the ultimate objective of all moral action and a person is under a moral obligation to achieve it. This obligation is not dictated by the will of God but by a person's own *reason*. As we have seen, a person should only perform actions that can be universalized without contradiction, as acting in this way is rational. It is irrational and immoral, on the other hand, to indulge in practices, such as lying, that cannot be universalized.

Now, a person can only be under the rational-moral obligation to achieve the *summum bonum* if it is *possible* to achieve it. Kant argues that *ought* implies *can*, that a person can only be under a moral obligation to achieve something if it is logically possible to do so. He believes that it is logically possible for a person to achieve the *summum bonum*, but not necessarily in one lifetime. Practical difficulties mean that while a person can achieve virtue in this world, it is beyond their power to ensure that their virtue is rewarded with happiness.

A look at the world reveals that there are some virtuous people who are not happy, perhaps because they suffer pain and abuse, and that there are certainly many other people who are happy, at least in some sense of the word, but not virtuous. In order for it to be logically possible to achieve the *summum bonum*, to achieve the coincidence of virtue and happiness, in order for there to be a genuine moral obligation to *strive* to achieve it in this life, it must be possible to achieve it after death.

God must exist, argues Kant, as he is the only being capable of facilitating, in some kind of heaven, the eventual harmonization of virtue and happiness that morality aims at and requires. Kant endorsed what is called the *moral argument* for God's existence while rejecting the rest.

In a nutshell Kant is saying there is no guarantee of justice in this world. The virtuous are not necessarily rewarded with the happiness that ought to complement their virtue. Therefore, there must be the God-given guarantee of justice in the next world.

In a sense, Kant's position is comparable to that of Buddhism which recognizes that the highest good, the state of perfect blessedness or bliss known as *nirvana*, is not achievable in one lifetime. What the Buddhists claim must be achieved over many lifetimes, through many reincarnations, Kant claims must be achieved in the hereafter.

Kant was a devout Christian, but his motive in formulating this argument was perhaps not so much to endorse a broadly Christian world-view, as to rescue human existence from a kind of *moral futility* in which it ultimately makes no difference whether one strives to live the life of Robert Mugabe or Mother Teresa, Muammar Gaddafi or Mahatma Gandhi, John Willoughby or Elinor Dashwood.

Some critics of Kant argue that although his moral theory provides precise guidance on how to behave on each and every occasion, although it leaves no moral grey areas, it is for these very reasons entirely *inflexible*. This criticism is unfair, not least because it ignores the important distinction Kant draws between perfect and imperfect duties which we covered earlier and about which he has a great deal to say. As said, imperfect duties are indeterminate, they can be fulfilled in various ways and so permit a considerable degree of flexibility.

Although there is far more flexibility in Kant's moral theory than his least generous and subtle critics give him credit for, he nonetheless shows himself to be inflexible in his insistence that truth-telling is always a perfect duty; that there are no specific situations, or peculiar types of situation, in which lying is permissible.

Many critics of Kant have long argued that surely it is right, for example, to lie from altruistic motives. A terrified man is pursued by an axe-wielding psychopath intent on splitting his skull. The man finds his way to your door and pleads for sanctuary. You allow him to hide under your floorboards, or in your garden shed if you are reluctant to rip up those nice fitted carpets. When the axe-wielding psychopath knocks on your door, demanding to know where the man is, surely it is right and proper for you to throw the lunatic off his intended victim's trail with a string of outright fibs, lies and porky pies, rather than slavishly adhere to the categorical imperative and tell him the truth.

Surely, it is intuitively obvious, so to speak, that your response ought to be to take the liberty of deceiving him. It is surely what any sensible, down-to-earth, decent sort of person capable of compassion, empathy and fellow feeling would do. What would you do?

Kant, of course, light years more logical even than Spock, will have no truck with the claim that it is all right to lie from altruistic motives, and says so quite clearly in a famous paper he wrote called 'On a Supposed Right to Lie from Altruistic Motives' (1799), these days often given the equally snappy title 'On a Supposed Right to Lie because of Philanthropic Concerns'.

In a sense it is regrettable that Kant wrote this short paper at all –
although it is undoubtedly invaluable for stimulating informative debate
– as it is now too often used against him by those more interested in
mocking and belittling him for probably the most questionable thing he
ever wrote than praising him for the great many brilliant things he wrote.

Anyway, in 'On a Supposed Right to Lie from Altruistic Motives'
Kant argues, in so many words, that a man who lies to an axe-wielding
psychopath may well do no harm to the axe man himself, but
nonetheless his lies are harmful in a broader sense because they do
their bit to undermine the principle of truth-telling upon which contracts,
the law and the whole operation of human society is based.

The maxim established by his lies, that it is ok for everyone to lie on
certain occasions, is a move towards creating a world in which true
declarations are met with incredulity not credence. A world where no
one believed anything anyone said would be a terrible, anarchic place.
A place, interestingly, where it would not even be possible to tell lies for
altruistic or any other motives because lies only succeed where there
is trust to be betrayed.

> And even though by telling an untruth I do no wrong to him who
> unjustly compels me to make a statement, yet by this falsification,
> which as such can be called a lie (though not in a juridical sense), I
> do wrong to duty in general in a most essential point. That is, as far
> as in me lies I bring it about that statements (declarations) in general
> find no credence, and hence also that all rights based on contracts
> become void and lose their force, and this is a wrong done to
> mankind in general.
>
>   'On a Supposed Right to Lie because of
>   Philanthropic Concerns', p. 64

As ever, Kant offers a forceful argument. Nonetheless, the charge
against him is not entirely dismissed: that here at least he is out of
touch with everyday reality, that he unpragmatically insists on placing
a highly abstract, inflexible moral principle above common sense and

common decency. A strict Kantian who gave Jews away to Nazis because he refused to lie about where they were hiding does not appear to be a moral man but rather a hopelessly moralistic one, a sort of moral monster.

Of course, it is worth noting that you could avoid lying to the axe-wielding psychopath by meeting his demands with silence or with an honest refusal to tell him what he wants to know, although it is perhaps not prudent to suggest to psychopaths that you know what they want to know but are not prepared to tell them.

A wiser approach is to cunningly mislead without actually lying, as did Saint Athanasius. In his book *The Virtues* (p. 115), Peter Geach tells how Saint Athanasius once encountered Roman soldiers intent on killing him. Not recognizing him, they asked, 'Where is the traitor Athanasius?' Mindful that he should not lie, but also that he did not have a duty to give himself over to those intent on murdering him, Athanasius was inspired by God to answer, 'Not far away'. As a result, the soldiers departed and Athanasius escaped.

It seems we dare not behave as perfectly as Kant proposes because the human world is not perfectly good, but the human world is not perfectly good because we do not all behave, all of the time, as Kant proposes. If we did all consistently behave as Kant proposes, his kingdom of ends would be realized and there would be no murdering Nazis or Roman soldiers tempting us to lie.

The debate continues and will probably never be finally resolved, but certainly there are alternative moral theories to Kant's that offer seemingly plausible support to the pragmatic claim that there are occasions when lying, stealing and even murder are morally right. One such theory is *utilitarianism*, which we will now explore.

Goodness and Happiness

Utilitarianism is a *consequentialist* moral theory. Unlike Kant's deontological or duty-based ethics, utilitarianism judges the rightness or wrongness of actions by an empirical assessment of their consequences; an empirical, broadly scientific assessment of their *utility* or usefulness. The definition of *empirical* is: based on, concerned with, or verifiable by observation or experience rather than theory or pure logic.

Utilitarianism is a moral theory very much rooted in the Anglo-Saxon *empiricist* tradition of John Locke and David Hume, two philosophical giants who both reject *a priori* and metaphysical reasoning as a basis for human knowledge in favour of sensory experience. Empiricist thinking during the eighteenth-century *Age of Enlightenment* gave a huge boost to the observational and experimental sciences that have so transformed the human world since. The human world has also been transformed by the influence of empiricism in general, and utilitarianism in particular, upon the way many people now think about morality and the nature of goodness.

The greatest English philosopher of them all, John Locke, argues throughout his highly influential major work *An Essay Concerning Human Understanding* (1689) that there are no innate principles in the mind, that at birth the mind is a *tabula rasa* (a blank slate).

For his part, the greatest Scottish philosopher of them all, David Hume, argues throughout his own equally influential major work *A Treatise of Human Nature* (1738), a work heavily influenced by Locke, that we have no simple *ideas* in our minds that are not derived from simple sensory *impressions*. For example, a person who has never seen yellow can have no idea of yellow. A complex idea of something we have never seen, a centaur for example, is a combination of simple ideas derived from simple impressions.

The complete rejection of innate principles and *a priori* ideas so clearly heard in the philosophies of Locke and Hume is loudly echoed by the chief exponent of utilitarianism, the nineteenth-century English philosopher John Stuart Mill. In advancing a wholly secular moral theory Mill meticulously avoids any appeal to religious, metaphysical or abstract reasoning in formulating its principles. As he says, 'It is proper to state that I forgo any advantage which could be derived to my argument from the idea of abstract right, as a thing independent of utility' (*On Liberty*, p. 15).

Every philosopher is influenced and inspired by those philosophers who came before him or her, so much so that it is impossible to say where any idea truly began. There were doubtless Neolithic cave dwellers who were broadly utilitarian in their approach to morality, quite simply because the long-term survival of any tribe depends on its members tending to perform actions that are of utility to the group as a whole. Ethics can get very complicated, but at heart it is concerned with the common-sense rules that make social life possible and bearable. In conjunction with law, which is informed by it and which often enforces its core principles, ethics facilitates harmonious social interaction as oil enables an engine not only to run but to run smoothly.

As a distinctly structured and propounded moral theory, however, utilitarianism can be traced back to its founding father, the English philosopher and social reformer Jeremy Bentham, whose auto-icon is on permanent display at University College London. That is, his preserved skeleton padded out with straw and suitably clothed. His head is preserved also, but is kept locked away largely because it looks so macabre. The auto-icon has a wax head complete with some of Bentham's hair.

Bentham fought for social reform in many areas but his particular focus was the criminal law which he criticized vehemently. In 1780 he wrote *An Introduction to the Principles of Morals and Legislation* in which he sets out the core principles of utilitarianism while dismissing the notion of *absolute* moral rights and duties. He argues that rights and duties exist only within a manmade legal framework. Thus, he dismisses any notion of *natural* rights and duties as fundamental principles that exist outside or prior to the establishment of a civil society, be they supposedly God given or rooted in supposed laws of nature.

For Bentham, *utility* is the sole basis of morality and the key question to ask regarding the morality of any human action is, 'Does this action tend to promote happiness?' Bentham equates happiness with pleasure and the absence of pain. He is, therefore, very much a *hedonist*.

The most common use of the term *hedonist* evokes images of a party animal in constant and enthusiastic pursuit of sex, drugs and rock and roll, but more generally the term simply means 'the pursuit of pleasure', whatever that pleasure may be, a nice cup of tea and a good book as much as five ecstasy tabs and an orgy.

Bentham was a *psychological* and *ethical hedonist*. He held that humans are psychologically hardwired to desire pleasure and that it is therefore our fundamental moral obligation to maximize it. It may seem that it is most moral to pursue ecstasy tabs and orgies as these things appear to involve maximum pleasure, but the downside also has to be taken into account: the risk of drug overdose and sexually transmitted diseases, for example, pains not attendant upon a nice cup of tea and a good book.

Moderate pleasures tend not to have a dark side, are easier to obtain, can be enjoyed more frequently and, though less intense, are often of longer duration. A nice cup of tea and a good book can be enjoyed every day, several times a day if you are really self-indulgent, without harm to oneself or others, whereas a life of drugs and orgies is destined in the end to take its toll on health, relationships and finances.

For proof of this claim watch almost any one of those rock-star rockumentaries in which famous musicians tread that well-worn path from youthful optimism and creativity, to superstardom, to a little something to keep them going after the gig, to repeated visits to rehab, to choking to death on their own vomit in the penthouse of a Las Vegas hotel while attempting to snort cocaine from the thighs of a bevy of high-class call girls. Rock and roll suicide may sound like 'the way to go' but it probably isn't.

With the comparative measure of different pleasures and pains in mind Bentham formulated an algorithm, the *felicific* or *hedonic calculus*. *Felicific* means *happiness-making*, and in considering what makes us happy he reasoned much as we did above, that the greatness of a pleasure, or indeed a pain, is not simply a matter of its intensity. Bentham's felicific calculus includes seven vectors:

1 *Intensity*: How intense is the pleasure or pain?

2 *Duration*: How long does the pleasure or pain last?

3 *Certainty*: What is the probability of the pleasure or pain occurring?

4 *Propinquity*: How soon will the pleasure or pain occur?

5 *Fecundity*: What is the probability of the pleasure being followed by further pleasures, the pain by further pains?

6 *Purity*: What is the probability of the pleasure being followed by pains, the pain by pleasures?

7 *Extent*: How many persons will be affected by the pleasure or pain?

Bentham is criticized for considering pleasure only *quantitatively* and not also *qualitatively*, a shortcoming in his utilitarianism that his protégé John Stuart Mill overcomes with his distinction between higher and lower pleasures.

As we will see, John Stuart Mill also refined Bentham's utilitarianism in other important ways in order to render the general theory of utilitarianism more sensible and workable. The moral theory of utilitarianism achieved its highest expression in the work of John Stuart Mill who, in aligning it closely with his influential theory of liberalism, became the most influential English philosopher of the nineteenth century, second only to Locke as the greatest English philosopher of them all.

Being social reformers, Bentham and John Stuart Mill's father, James Mill, another major exponent of the creed of utilitarianism, valued education very highly as a key vehicle of social reform. As a result, little John Stuart became the subject of an intensive learning programme that had him studying Greek by the age of three and Plato's dialogues by the age of eight.

Above all, they wanted to create a genius who would pick up the reins of utilitarianism and drive it forward after they were dead and one of them at least was buried. John Stuart did not disappoint and in time went on to re-evaluate the rather narrow, unsophisticated principles of Benthamism to produce a more subtle, less dogmatic, less mathematical utilitarianism that recognizes that individual liberties must not be swept aside in the drive for social reform.

An accomplished logician, that's *logician* not magician – magic and logic could not be further apart – Mill wrote *A System of Logic* (1843) before turning his attention to political philosophy. His seminal essay *On Liberty* (1859) is arguably the most brilliant and eloquent defence of liberal and democratic principles ever written. No ivory tower philosopher, Mill followed his father and Bentham in practising what he preached. He campaigned for social reform on many fronts, including, as Member of Parliament for Westminster from 1865 to 1868, votes for women.

Following Bentham, Mill argues that if an action contributes to the sum total of human happiness it is a morally good action. If it contributes to the reverse of happiness, to the sum total of human suffering, it is a morally bad action. This is Mill's 'Greatest Happiness Principle', the central pillar of his utilitarianism, which he summed up as follows in his powerful essay of 1861, *Utilitarianism*:

> The creed which accepts as the foundation of morals, Utility, or the Greatest Happiness Principle, holds that actions are right in proportion as they tend to promote happiness, wrong as they tend to produce the reverse of happiness. By happiness is intended pleasure, and the absence of pain; by unhappiness, pain, and the privation of pleasure.
>
> *Utilitarianism*, p. 137, in *On Liberty and Other Essays*

For Mill, the only real measure of moral goodness is what tends to make reasonably well-adjusted people happy: the absence of pain, physical and mental pleasure, decent food, sanitation, shelter, respect from others, friends, something creative and constructive to do and so on.

Mill argues, quite sensibly, that to discover what makes people happy you only have to look at what it is most people the world over want and have always wanted. As was said when we considered the *golden rule* of treat others as you would have them treat you, most people want only what is, broadly speaking, pleasant. If they do not, if they want to be tortured and abused for example, then there is something warped about them. We could say that such warped people – Brandes, the willing victim of the Rotenburg Cannibal for instance, not to mention the Rotenburg Cannibal himself – no longer really know what they want.

Up to this point in the account, Mill's position is not really distinguishable from Bentham's. Beyond it, however, they begin to part company. Mill criticizes Bentham for tending to equate happiness with bodily pleasure and for placing all pleasures on the same mathematical scale, for lumping the trivial game of push-pin in with poetry, for thinking that all diverse pleasures can be likewise crunched through his felicific grinder and assigned a value in *hedons* at the end of the process.

In *The Rationale of Reward* (1825, p. 206) Bentham writes, 'Prejudice aside, the game of push-pin is of equal value with the arts and sciences of music and poetry. If the game of push-pin furnish more pleasure, it is more valuable than either.' As said, for his part, Mill argues that pleasures are not just *quantitatively* different, but *qualitatively* different as well, implying that some pleasures are of a *superior quality* to others; implying, for example, that at least some music and poetry, 'the best' music and poetry, is intrinsically more valuable than push-pin.

Being a more subtle thinker than Bentham, Mill sees the need to distinguish between *higher* and *lower* pleasures. Mill argues that people who are capable of experiencing both higher and lower pleasures, and have genuinely done so, know that higher pleasures are more valuable and rewarding than lower pleasures, that higher pleasures are qualitatively superior. Moreover, they would not forgo the possibility of experiencing higher pleasures in exchange for the maximum bovine contentment of the utterly satisfied ignoramus.

They would not, for example, exchange the greater quality of pleasure to be had from listening to Mozart or reading Keats for a daily supply of the world's best ice cream, although a person not forced to choose one over the other could listen to Mozart and read Keats *while* eating the world's best ice cream. Not too much of it though, as it will make them sick, the ice cream that is, not Mozart or Keats.

A few of those forced to study Keats at school might beg to differ, although the immortal opening line of Keats's deep and lengthy poem *Endymion* surely concurs with Mill's position: 'A thing of beauty is a joy forever' (*Endymion*, Book I, in *The Complete Poems of John Keats*). Mill was a big fan of poetry, particularly Wordsworth and Coleridge. Bentham was not so keen. In his 1838 essay on Bentham, Mill attributes to him the dismissive aphorism, 'All poetry is misrepresentation' (*Bentham*, in *Mill on Bentham and Coleridge*, p. 95).

Even by a Benthamite measure, listening to Mozart or reading Keats are clearly *purer* pleasures than eating ice cream, as there is a far higher probability that eating a lot of ice cream will lead to pain than there is that listening to a lot of Mozart or Keats will lead to pain.

Only higher pleasures engage and satisfy the higher faculties that distinguish humans from the rest of the animal kingdom. A dog, unlike a cow or a slug, has a love of excitement, but that love is easily satisfied with a walk or a thrown ball. Although in its own way a dog may enjoy going on holiday or skydiving, a dog does not *crave* the excitement of them as humans do.

As to the even more subtle thrills of reading Jane Austen or playing chess, these are totally alien to all non-human animals, however bright and emotionally intelligent some are in their own way, because far outside of their specific cognitive capacities. If your dog looks sad today, you can rest assured it is not because he has misplaced his copy of *Pride and Prejudice*.

Some non-human animals build nests or burrows according to their instincts but no animal is creative in the way humans are. Not everyone is Leonardo da Vinci but most humans enjoy being creative on some level and suffer psychologically and even physically when every opportunity to be creative is denied them. Mill says:

> Now it is an unquestionable fact that those who are equally acquainted with, and equally capable of appreciating and enjoying both, do give a most marked preference to the manner of existence which employs their higher faculties. Few human creatures would consent to be changed into any of the lower animals, for a promise of the fullest allowance of a beast's pleasures; no intelligent human being would consent to be a fool, no instructed person would be an ignoramus, no person of feeling and conscience would be selfish and base, even though they should be persuaded that the fool, the dunce, or the rascal is better satisfied with his lot than they are with theirs.
>
> *Utilitarianism*, p. 139, in *On Liberty and Other Essays*

Mill argues that most humans would rather suffer a level of discontent in pursuit of the happiness which only the engagement of their higher faculties can bring about than be content with what satisfies a pig.

Many people, for example, suffer greatly in pursuit of true love, are repeatedly hurt and disappointed along the way, but it would not make them happy to give up their romantic quest in exchange for seeking to content themselves with being single, especially if that meant wallowing on the sofa night after night overdosing on chocolate while watching *Celebrity Big Brother*. In order to become content with being single they would somehow have to lose a higher part of who they are, the part that craves the higher emotional pleasures of companionship, intimacy and romance.

Mill argues that we should not confuse happiness with contentment, and in doing so famously concludes that it is better to be a dissatisfied human being with the capacity to appreciate higher pleasures than a satisfied pig with no capacity to appreciate higher pleasures:

Whoever supposes that this preference [for higher pleasures] takes place at a sacrifice of happiness – that the superior being, in anything like equal circumstances, is not happier than the inferior – confounds the two very different ideas, of happiness, and content. It is indisputable that the being whose capacities of enjoyment are low, has the greatest chance of having them fully satisfied; and a highly endowed being will always feel that any happiness which he can look for, as the world is constituted, is imperfect. But he can learn to bear its imperfections, if they are at all bearable; and they will not make him envy the being who is indeed unconscious of the imperfections, but only because he feels not at all the good which those imperfections qualify. It is better to be a human being dissatisfied than a pig satisfied; better to be Socrates dissatisfied than a fool satisfied. And if the fool, or the pig, are of a different opinion, it is because they only know their own side of the question. The other party to the comparison knows both sides.

Utilitarianism, p. 140, in *On Liberty and Other Essays*

Like a great many philosophers, whatever their specific school of thought, Mill equates moral goodness with happiness. What is morally good is to strive for a world where happiness is maximized, not only for oneself, but as far as is reasonably possible for others as well, not least because it is difficult to be happy when those close to us are seriously unhappy. The focus for philosophers interested in the difference between right and wrong and the true nature of goodness almost inevitably shifts towards working out the true nature of happiness, not least because understanding what goodness is requires understanding what its ultimate *goal* is.

At times I feel I could have subtitled this book *How to Be Happy*, it being the case that any book about goodness will inevitably drift towards being a book about happiness to a significant degree. Certainly, the theme of happiness and what happiness truly is will emerge again, particularly when we explore the virtue ethics of Aristotle.

It has already been said that Kantian ethics is concerned with duty while utilitarianism is concerned with consequences. In further comparing the two theories it can be said that utilitarianism is perhaps easier to grasp than Kantian ethics because it is a far less abstract, far more down-to-earth, practical theory. However, it can lack precision. Whereas Kant is very clear about what you should not do, Mill and company have to constantly play the rather tedious game of assessing the consequences of actions and types of action to see if they add to or detract from the sum total of human happiness.

Sometimes it is easy to see that an action, a rape for example, causes a vast amount of suffering and misery and only provides a sick, temporary pleasure to the scumbag who perpetrates it. But often it is not so easy to decide if an action will, on balance, produce more happiness than unhappiness. Buying expensive drugs to help a cancer patient will obviously produce happiness for the patient and his family, but what if the same money could be spent saving the lives of fifty babies who will otherwise die?

The ideal solution, of course, is to save the cancer patient *and* the babies but in the real world resources are always limited. A strong case can always be made to increase spending on any health service in the world, and probably some wealthy nations could afford to double their health spending, all be it with extensive economic restructuring that is likely to have a detrimental effect in other areas. But even if they did so, there would still be things they could not afford to do, there would still be difficult either–or decisions to be made, especially given the many miraculous but highly expensive cures now available thanks to scientifically advanced medicines, technologies and procedures.

In order to provide a means of solving at least some of the difficulties involved in deciding if an action, on balance, produces more happiness than unhappiness, Mill, in further refining utilitarianism, introduced the crucially important distinction between *act* and *rule* utilitarianism.

Act utilitarianism claims that each particular action should be evaluated individually in terms of its actual consequences. The problem with act utilitarianism is that it is often difficult, even impossible, to judge what the consequences of a particular action will be. Also, it is too permissive, in that it can be used to justify any particular action if the consequences of that particular action can be said to have somehow contributed to the greatest happiness, even if it was the kind of action, such as slaughtering children, that generally and as a rule produces great suffering.

Rule utilitarianism aims to overcome the shortcomings of act utilitarianism. Rather than focus on the utility of particular actions, rule utilitarianism focuses on the utility of rules prescribing *types* of action. A rule is of utility if following it tends to promote the greatest happiness more than not following it; if it is judged probable rather than improbable, on the basis of past experience, that following the rule will promote the greatest happiness. For a rule utilitarian, a morally right action is one that is in accordance with such a rule.

Not slaughtering children, for example, tends to promote the greatest happiness. Therefore, even on those rare occasions when slaughtering children would somehow have significant positive consequences, the morally right thing to do would be to stick to the rule and not slaughter the children.

Rule utilitarianism is a far better guide to action than act utilitarianism because it formally allows previous experience of likely consequences to be taken into consideration, whereas act utilitarianism does not. It also offers protection to vulnerable individuals and minorities threatened by the demands of the majority. Mill's more refined brand of utilitarianism certainly champions the cause of individuals and minorities.

In *On Liberty*, Mill advocates that individuals and minorities should be free to think, speak and act as they please, so long as their opinions and way of life do not harm others. This has come to be known as Mill's *harm principle*: 'The only purpose for which power can be rightfully exercised over any member of a civilised community, against his will, is to prevent harm to others. His own good, either physical or moral, is not a sufficient warrant' (*On Liberty*, p. 14).

For example, according to Mill, the authorities have no right to prevent a recreational drug user from taking recreational drugs or to punish him for doing so, unless his habit is causing harm to others. The extent to which the use of recreational drugs harms others, and the circumstances under which it does and does not harm others, are a matter of heated debate confused by prejudice on both sides, debate I shall resist exploring here as I have other medicines to mix.

For Mill, liberty of thought, expression and action, so long as it does not harm others, is the cornerstone of a truly civilized society. A society that lacks such liberties, for whatever reason, is primitive and backward. His utilitarian justification for valuing liberty so highly is that personal freedom is so pleasing to most people, so essential to their feeling that they are fully functioning human beings, rather than mere satisfied pigs shut in a sty, that they simply cannot be happy without it.

Cruder forms of utilitarianism appear to justify riding roughshod over individuals and minorities if doing so benefits the majority. The blunt argument goes that if a new road, for example, will improve transport links for thousands of people and boost the national economy, then it is just tough luck for the relatively few people who will be adversely affected by the building of the new road. Transport infrastructure, of course, has to develop. Our modern, technological, consumer society, from which we all benefit in many ways, simply could not function, indeed would not have developed in the first place, if our transport system was still based on the rutted track and the horse drawn cart.

Road planners, however, need to be subtle utilitarians. They have to consider whether or not the proposed new road is really needed, whether or not there is an alternative route less damaging to local residents and the local environment and so on. At the very least, they have to mitigate as far as possible the negative impacts of the new road on those living near it, and relocate and compensate those who must be moved. Fortunately, in any civilized, democratic, tolerant, liberal society there will be a reasonable amount of legislation to make sure these measures are enacted, although to some extent there will still always be winners and losers.

Resisting the tyranny of the majority and taking care of minorities, be they ethnic, religious or just a bunch of so-called nimbies concerned about having their pleasant way of life trashed by fracking, is entirely in keeping with the principles of a more refined utilitarianism. The simple reason being that no one can feel at all relaxed, secure and ultimately happy in a society where at any moment their minority or individual desires, hopes and aspirations can be completely disregarded in favour of the hopes and desires of the majority.

To employ an extreme example to further illustrate the point, the crudest act utilitarianism allows that it is good, because useful to society, i.e. of utility, to kill a healthy tramp in order to use his vital organs to save the life of several Nobel Prize winning scientists. The tiny downside will be one dead tramp with no real friends who was of no use to society alive, while the huge upside will be the survival of several geniuses who will go on to invent all sorts of goodies of far-reaching benefit to humankind.

The problem with all this, however, is: who would seriously want to live in a society where their vital organs could be seized by the authorities if they fell below a certain level of income or usefulness? And who would want this to happen to their nearest and dearest, however poor and useless they were? Such a society would not be at ease with itself. Indeed, terror would stalk its streets.

The same can be said for a society that terminated its old people regardless of whether or not they wanted to go on living. There are doubtless all sorts of practical and financial advantages to culling old people once they retire and especially once they become a burden on younger relatives and social services. Certainly, extermination of the elderly would solve the housing shortage at a stroke. Admittedly, a lot of people are employed in caring for the elderly but surely the loss of that employment would be more than offset by the huge sums of money freed up by getting rid of old, inconvenient buffers and biddies.

But who, young or old, could be happy in such a society? Not least, everyone would dread for decades in advance whatever day was fixed for their certain execution. And if no day was fixed, everyone would dread reaching a certain level of infirmity and dependence even more than they do now. Who would do the killing? How would the killing be done? What sort of pernicious lies and myths would have to be disseminated to make people accept their dire fate more readily? For more on all this check out the 1976 film *Logan's Run*, which portrays a twenty-third-century dystopia in which resources have become so scarce that citizens are terminated at the tender age of thirty.

Act utilitarianism, in advocating the slaughter of innocents if it should benefit the majority, severely lacks a sense of *justice*. It is just not fair to murder an innocent child, however much doing so might benefit the human race in some weird scenario I will leave you to dream up for yourself. Utilitarianism, of course, does not allow for *fairness* as a moral principle in its own right. Utilitarianism can only consider the *consequences* of fairness, otherwise it is straying from the key principles that define it.

Fortunately, rule utilitarianism, in recognizing that *as a rule* slaughtering children does not contribute to the general happiness, and that therefore it should not be done even on those rare occasions when it would somehow have significant positive consequences, restores a sense of justice to utilitarianism. That is, justice in the broad sense of having social rules that contribute to the general happiness because they are fair and reasonable to all, rather than justice understood as an abstract principle derived from religious or metaphysical reasoning.

Utilitarianism is essentially a sensible and practical moral theory occupying a prime position in the everyday ethical toolkit of many individuals, groups and organizations. As said, however, utilitarianism can lack precision and at its worst it is a pretty blunt instrument. Rule utilitarianism is undoubtedly the most important sharpening of that instrument. Indeed, arguably, the theory soon becomes unworkable without it.

As utilitarianism has developed, further variants of it have emerged as moral philosophers have considered the definitions of pleasure and suffering, the consequences of actions and types of action and the complex nature of happiness.

These variants seek to make utilitarianism a more valid, relevant and applicable moral theory by providing clearer answers to such familiar utilitarian questions as: How do we better judge what will be the outcome of particular actions? Do large amounts of happiness enjoyed by a few people outweigh small amounts of happiness enjoyed by a lot of people? Whose happiness do we take into account, everyone alive, future generations, even animals? Should one or a few individuals suffer for the happiness of the many? How do we take into account different tastes and preferences, the fact that one man's meat is another man's poison?

Modern-day utilitarians tend to prefer to be called *consequentialists*, arguing that the broader term *consequentialism* better covers the wide variety of so-called *variants of utilitarianism* now available. By way of concluding this section, some of the variants of *consequentialism* are outlined below.

As you will see, there is a degree of overlap between these variants and much of what they say will not be entirely new to you given what has already been covered. They are, after all, variants of a theory, not various departures from it. Arguably, they differ mainly in terms of emphasis, but certainly they all shed additional light on what consequentialism is about.

Negative utilitarianism values actions that *minimize* human suffering and misery. It recommends the *reduction of intrinsic disvalue*. That is, the reduction of those things that people find inherently unpleasant: hunger, lack of shelter, pain and so on. A key problem for negative utilitarianism is that one way to reduce human misery is to put everyone out of their misery by killing them.

Positive utilitarianism values actions that *maximize* human pleasure and happiness. It recommends the *maximization of intrinsic value*. That is, the maximization of those things that people find most pleasant. Like negative utilitarianism, it recognizes that minimizing suffering is important, but it also recognizes that people need more than the removal of hunger and pain to make them happy. That is, they need additional, positive benefits like friendship, respect, mental stimulation, challenges and so on.

Preference utilitarianism holds that the rightness of an action depends on the degree to which it satisfies a person's preferences. It holds that people cannot be happy unless they are able to satisfy at least some of their preferences. It recognizes that in the real world not all preferences can be satisfied on all occasions, particularly as the satisfaction of one person's preferences may well mean the serious dissatisfaction of the preferences of others.

To take a mundane example, as opposed to the grisly or even gristly example of a preference for consuming human flesh over beefsteak: Mr Toad's preference for parking his oversized 4×4 right outside the shop rather than in the car park, regardless of the fact that he is causing an obstruction, will detract from the preference of the majority to get about the streets.

Preference utilitarianism recognizes the inevitability of compromise, that we often have to be happy with, and often only in fact aim for, the partial satisfaction of our preferences. In his 1957 book *Models of Man: Social and Rational*, the Nobel Prize winning American political scientist, economist, psychologist and philosopher Herbert A. Simon names this partial satisfaction of preferences *satisfice*, as in, the level of satisfaction that will suffice. In his detailed studies of rational decision-making, Simon notes that often people do not seek the best outcome, they do not *optimize*. Instead, they tend to go in for *satisficing*, achieving an outcome that is *good enough*.

Ideal utilitarianism, as advocated by the mighty Cambridge ethicist George Edward Moore, better known as G. E. Moore, author of the seminal *Principia Ethica* (1903), seeks to be distinct from hedonistic utilitarianism. It denies that morality is concerned with maximizing pleasure and happiness. *Intrinsic value* belongs to friendship, aesthetic experience and so on. Such things, therefore, ought to be pursued and promoted for their own sake. *Intrinsic disvalue* belongs to disdain for beauty and to enjoyment of whatever is ugly, sordid, ignoble and so on. Such things, therefore, ought to be avoided and discouraged.

Ideal utilitarians appear to equate pleasure only with lower, bodily pleasures, resisting the use of the term *pleasure* with regard to anything more intellectual, artistic and refined. What ideal utilitarians resist referring to as *pleasures*, however, appear to be very similar to, if not the same as, Mill's *higher pleasures*. More from G. E. Moore in due course.

Finally, *indirect utilitarianism* argues that a person is more likely to choose those actions that promote the greatest happiness if he has developed certain *positive attitudes and character traits* than if he has not developed them and instead simply undertakes to weigh up possible outcomes each time he intends to act.

The claim is that for truly good people, who tend to quietly promote happiness wherever they go, there is no *deliberation* on their part as to how they should act. Doing the right thing has become *second nature* to them. Colonel Brandon, for example, in Austen's *Sense and Sensibility*, always acts with discretion, propriety, empathy and charity. These virtues seem to flow from his *general character*, rather than from case-by-case calculations as to what he should do for the best and how he should promote the common good.

Colonel Brandon has the advantage of being naturally strong-willed and temperate, not to mention the circumstantial advantage of being wealthy. Yet, if he is saintly, it is largely because life has taught him the constant perils of indiscreet and divisive gossip on the one hand, and the eternal value of good manners, judicious kindness and unpretentious generosity on the other. So much so that he no longer has to *contemplate* behaving accordingly, he just does it.

Aristotle's virtue theory also emphasizes the achievement of goodness and happiness through the development of certain positive attitudes and character traits. It is to Aristotle's moral theory that we now turn.

Goodness and the Golden Mean

Mention Aristotle to people and most of them will say, 'Who?' In a way this is strange because Aristotle's diverse theories dominated Western thinking in many disciplines for many centuries, from logic to drama, from physics to politics, from metaphysics to ethics. The world we live in today is still shaped in many subtle ways by his ideas, principles and categories. As you will have noticed, he has managed to find his way into this book several times already, before we even reached this chapter dedicated to him.

In terms of genius, Aristotle certainly grew to equal his master, Plato, and is the only philosopher to rival the vastness of Plato's influence on the history of ideas. Plato wins the photo finish on that score mainly because Aristotle was a product of Plato, and more specifically Plato's Academy, a school of philosophy founded by Plato in Athens in 387 BCE where Aristotle studied and taught for over eighteen years. Although he was Plato's head boy, Aristotle was no slave to Plato's thinking. Like all good pupils, he modified and developed some of his master's ideas while rejecting others.

Most of those people you mention Aristotle to who *have* heard of him will immediately recite a famous line from Monty Python's *Bruces' Philosophers Song*, a comic ditty in which an impressive line-up of heavyweight thinkers are all accused of heavy alcohol consumption. The line refers to Aristotle's deep obsession with the bottle. The inspiration for the line is little more than the fact that 'Aristotle' rhymes with 'bottle', but it is nonetheless cleverly *ironic*, given that at its heart Aristotle's moral theory recommends moderation in all things, including liquor, an irony surely not lost on the Oxbridge swats of the Monty Python team.

Aristotle wrote extensively on ethics, producing, above all, the *Nicomachean Ethics*, possibly named after his son Nicomachus, who may have edited it, or possibly after his father Nicomachus, to whom it may have been dedicated. The *Nicomachean Ethics* is generally held to be Aristotle's most accomplished and important work on ethics and is certainly the most widely read and studied today.

He also wrote the *Eudemian Ethics*, named after his pupil Eudemus of Rhodes, who edited it. There is also the *Magna Moralia* and *On Virtues and Vices*. After long dispute amongst scholars, most now agree that these last two works were not written by Aristotle himself, but are rather faithful summaries of his views written by early followers.

Aristotle's earliest followers are known as the *Peripatetic school*, in memory of Aristotle's fondness for walking about the Lyceum (the temple of Apollo Lyceus in Athens) while he taught his classes. Walking goes well with thinking and talking, except when negotiating heavy traffic, which is just as well because in attending an Aristotle lecture a student had literally to follow the teacher while keeping up both physically and mentally. The *Nicomachean Ethics* is based on Aristotle's Lyceum lecture notes.

Aristotle is definitely one of those great philosophers ultimately in search of an ethics. He fathoms out this, that and the other to the nth degree in order to decide how we should live given what we know about what there is. In some ways, he *is* a lifestyle guru, offering people broad advice on how they should live and conduct themselves in all areas of their existence in order to get the most out of it, in order to reach their full potential as human beings, in order to flourish and achieve true happiness.

Quite a few scholars say that Aristotle's *Nicomachean Ethics* was originally intended as a sort of lifestyle and etiquette guide for ancient Greek aristocrats. There is undoubtedly some truth in this claim and certainly history reveals that many of the top people back then, as now, desperately needed the kind of sound advice Aristotle was offering on how to behave better.

Whatever audience Aristotle was writing for at the time, however, much of his guidance is undoubtedly still relevant to everyone alive today, regardless of their age, gender, race, religion, social status or number of Twitter followers. Many generations down through the centuries have found valuable advice in Aristotle's moral theory and it is not for nothing that his legacy has stood the test of time so well.

There are, nonetheless, elements of Aristotle's moral theory that, to a modern mind stuffed with Christian, Kantian, democratic and socialist notions of equality, justice and pity, sound at best strange and at worst rather shocking.

To begin to get to grips with Aristotle, it has to be understood that he was a master of logic. Among the many principles of logic that he established he warned against what is called *bad induction*, making a universal claim on the basis of too few particular instances. Just as I cannot claim that summer has arrived because I observe one swallow in the sky, so I cannot claim I am happy because I experience a temporary state of pleasure. 'One swallow does not make a summer; neither does one day. Similarly neither can one day, or a brief space of time, make a man blessed and happy' (*Nicomachean Ethics*, 1098a8–27, p. 76).

Aristotle is making the all-important point that happiness is not a fleeting sensation, but a sustained mode of existence bound up with a person's way of life, their regular actions, habits and attitudes and the way these shape their overall character.

Like Plato before him, Aristotle is keen to stress that true happiness and fulfilment are distinct from pleasure. A happy person takes pleasure in many things, but his happiness is not synonymous with the pleasure he takes. The relentless pursuit of pleasure leads to dissatisfaction, as a person cannot always get what he desires and will crave more and more of what he desires in order to achieve temporary satiation.

Not least, excessive pleasure, overindulgence, often leads to pain: sunburn, hangover, obesity, STDs. Similar points were raised when we considered Bentham's views on pleasure. Happiness, for Aristotle, is not just about what a person feels, or what they acquire, it is a whole way of being, a whole way of life.

Plato is something of an ascetic. He thinks that true happiness is to be found in a life of philosophical and spiritual contemplation where a person avoids riding the pleasure–pain roller coaster of physical indulgence. Like Plato, Aristotle also recognizes the value of philosophical and spiritual contemplation and sees it as an essential feature of the life of the person who is truly happy.

Looking to define human beings to the exclusion of all else, Aristotle said, 'Man is a rational animal.' Therefore, for a person to reason, contemplate and philosophize is for him to fulfil his true nature. The most successful person, for Aristotle, is one who can afford to spend his life philosophizing and meditating.

Aristotle was a pre-Christian pagan, and certainly no egalitarian. The contemplative life is not for everyone. It is only for those who are capable of aspiring to it by virtue of their social class, breeding, upbringing and education. As good, modern, democratic liberals, taught to value equal opportunities, this sounds very wrong to us, but the ancient Greeks did not share *our* notions of individualism, equality and justice.

For them, the good community is one in which everyone has their designated role within a rigid hierarchy, one in which everyone except the highest leader or leaders is fundamentally subordinate to someone else. Slaves are subordinate to women, women subordinate to their husbands, sons subordinate to their fathers, sisters subordinate to their brothers and so on. In his *History of Western Philosophy* (1945), Bertrand Russell compares Aristotle's notion of the good community to a good orchestra. 'In an orchestra, the first violin is more important than the oboe, though both are necessary for the excellence of the whole' (*History of Western Philosophy*, p. 189).

Justice for the ancient Greeks was not about fairness and equality – the oboe somehow being equal to the first violin – but about each member of a community realizing their full potential *within* their designated role. Injustice and social discord arise when individuals cease to focus on dutifully perfecting their own role, and instead begin meddling in the roles of others and assuming the rights and privileges of others.

In his greatest dialogue, *The Republic*, primarily a consideration of the nature of justice and the just society, Plato defines justice as minding one's own business. 'When each of our three classes (businessmen, Auxiliaries and Guardians) does its own job and minds its own business, that, by contrast, is justice and makes our state just' (*The Republic*, 434c, p. 139).

For Aristotle, rights are proportionate to a person's social role and status. As Russell notes, 'A father can repudiate his son if he is wicked, but a son cannot repudiate his father' (*History of Western Philosophy*, p. 186). Within the social organism it is simply not the place of sons, in relation to their fathers, to repudiate their fathers. It would be acceptable for a son to repudiate his father if he, the son, was a magistrate, by banishing him, for example, so long as he was acting as a magistrate and not as a son. As a magistrate he has different duties, rights and privileges to those of a son and occupies a different position in the social hierarchy.

Ancient Greek ideas of designated social role, subordination and justice are certainly not above criticism. Some critics have argued that they simply served to maintain an iniquitous social system based on gross exploitation, particularly of women and slaves. We would need to know much more about ancient Greek culture to decide the extent to which such criticism is valid, and how far it oversimplifies the situation and views it through the lens of our modern sensibilities.

One has to keep in mind that perhaps the ancient Greek city states were simply not ready for, and therefore could not sustain, our modern, egalitarian moral principles. That perhaps the only alternative to the existing 'unfair' social order was anarchy, just as in certain parts of the Middle East the alternative to a social order based on brutal dictatorship has proved to be anarchy rather than functioning democracy.

On the other hand, in appraising ancient Greek culture, it should not be forgotten that ancient Athens was a democracy, indeed the so-called cradle of democracy. Admittedly, only a relatively small subclass of the entire population was entitled to vote, the male citizens, but considerable equality of status and civil authority attached to each. It is no small matter that ancient Athenian democracy stood, and continues to stand, as a model for emulation across a broader base.

So, I suddenly find myself mounting a defence of moral differences between cultures, so-called *ethical relativism*, having criticized it from a Kantian perspective earlier on. Perhaps it is the case that practices that were acceptable during one historical period, because only they allowed a society to function and survive under the material conditions of that historical period, are no longer acceptable anywhere today. We are returned once again to the concept of *moral progress*, but this time with more awareness of the difficulties and dangers of *forcing* moral progress upon nations and cultures.

The key point to draw from the above consideration is that Aristotle, like Plato before him, sees ethics as a function of politics. What is ethical for an individual is for him to excel in his social role, his role within the *polis* (city or body of citizens). The highest virtue is only for the few, for the movers and shakers of the polis, for only they are capable of achieving it and only they require it.

Aristotle has much to say about how leading figures in society ought to conduct themselves generally and in relation to their superiors – if they have any – their social and educational equals and their many inferiors. The top people in society should have *megalopsuchia*, which is translated as greatness of soul, magnanimity, proper pride or self-respect. Interestingly, for Aristotle, it would be unbecoming for a slave, for example, to have this virtue. In not befitting his rank, affecting *megalopsuchia* would render the slave conceited and ridiculous; it would not appear in him as a virtue.

The magnanimous *man* – not slave, humble person or woman, although there seems to be no good reason why these qualities could not belong to a woman of high social standing – is one who has achieved virtue in every aspect of his life and hence perfected his character to the level of greatness. The magnanimous man knows his own worth without being arrogant or vain. He is self-controlled, dignified and brave. He does not take silly risks, but will face great dangers without concern for his own survival because he knows that the life of a coward is not worth living.

'He is disposed to confer benefits, but is ashamed to accept them, because the one is the act of a superior and the other that of an inferior' (*Nicomachean Ethics*, 1124a23–b14, p. 156). He is not haughty towards the humble because it is vulgar to use one's strength against the weak. He will seek honours only where they are great, disdaining popular contests and despising, as beneath his dignity, honours conferred by ordinary people for trivial reasons. He is bound to be honest because 'caring less for the truth than for what people think is a mark of timidity' (*Nicomachean Ethics*, 1124b14–1125a4, p. 157).

He cannot bear dependence because to do so is servile. He does not make small talk or indulge in gossip. He rarely pays compliments and is only abusive when he means very deliberately to insult his enemies. 'He does not nurse resentment, because it is beneath a magnanimous man to remember things against people, especially wrongs; it is more like him to overlook them' (*Nicomachean Ethics*, 1124b14–1125a27, pp. 157–8).

> The accepted view of the magnanimous man is that his gait is measured, his voice deep, and his speech unhurried. For since he takes few things seriously, he is not excitable, and since he regards nothing as great, he is not highly strung; and those are the qualities that make for shrillness of voice and hastiness in movement.
>
> *Nicomachean Ethics*, 1125a5–27, p. 158

It is hard to imagine that a modern-day magnanimous man would be a Twitter-twonk or demean himself by using any form of trivial, gossiping, shrill, resentful, malicious, sanctimonious social media. He might occasionally email a good friend or a sworn enemy for a very specific purpose, keeping it brief and ideally having his secretary do the actual typing. He would definitely not be a mobile-phone fiddler addicted to texting or the latest silly app.

It is hard to sum up Aristotle's account of the magnanimous man because his description, his list, goes on for several pages, but you get the picture. Personally, I cannot help being reminded of a movie hero, particularly as portrayed in those ultimate cinematographic morality tales, Westerns. John Wayne or Clint Eastwood. 'A man's gotta do what a man's gotta do.' A line often attributed to John Wayne, but more the essence of various similar lines from Westerns about facing up to grim reality with resolve and equanimity.

For his part, Russell says of the magnanimous man:

> The best individual [the magnanimous man], as conceived by Aristotle, is a very different person from the Christian saint. He

should have proper pride, and not underestimate his own merits. He should despise whoever deserves to be despised. The description of the proud or magnanimous man is very interesting as showing the difference between pagan and Christian ethics, and the sense in which Nietzsche was justified in regarding Christianity as a slave-morality.

History of Western Philosophy, p. 187

In *On the Genealogy of Morals* (1887) and other works, Nietzsche contrasts the *slave-morality* of Christianity with the *master-morality* of the ancient Greeks and other pre-Christian cultures. Slave-morality values asceticism, humility and pity, while master-morality values strength, pride and nobility.

Slave-morality incorporates what Nietzsche calls the *ascetic ideal*, the valuing of self-repression and self-denial above self-expression and enjoyment. Energy is directed inwards, wasted on guilt and regret, on repressing the dynamic human spirit, rather than, as with the *noble ideal* of master-morality, directed outwards in self-actualization and living life to the full. 'The highest men act out their lives without keeping back any residue of inner experience' (Friedrich Nietzsche, *Human, All-too-Human*, Volume 2, *Assorted Opinions and Maxims*, p. 228).

Slave-morality suits cowardly, insipid, unoriginal, unimaginative, uncreative, sheep-like losers who, terrified of the harsh existential realities of life, simply want to lose themselves in the herd, sharing herd values, beliefs and hopes and unquestioningly following herd rules. 'Morality is herd instinct in the individual' (Friedrich Nietzsche, *The Gay Science*, Book 3, p. 116).

At the heart of slave-morality is *ressentiment*, feelings of envy and hatred towards those who are perceived to be to blame for one's frustrations, frequently those who live according to master-morality. *Ressentiment* involves blaming others for one's difficulties, regardless of whether or not they are really to blame, and refusing to accept any personal responsibility for one's inadequacies and problems or for the overcoming of one's inadequacies and problems.

Ressentiment involves the false, jealous-minded belief that the success of one person can only ever be achieved at the expense of another. That the only way to prevent life from being this perceived *zero sum game* is for everyone to be somehow permanently equalized, regardless of individual talent, effort or prudence, or indeed, individual incompetence, indolence and recklessness.

Slave-morality, then, is a means by which the weak and mean-spirited collectively seek to undermine strong and magnanimously spirited individuals, mainly by conniving to fill them with guilt and regret about their strong appetites, natural advantages, personal achievements and proper pride.

Ironically, the mean-spiritedness of slave-morality is revealed by the fact that it treats *pity* as a virtue. In truth, pity is a cunningly spiteful way of feeling superior to others and one of the profoundest insults one person can pay another. Interestingly, the term 'pity' derives from the Latin term 'pietas', which means duty. The terms 'piety' and 'pious' often imply 'sanctimonious', 'holier-than-thou', 'smug' or even 'condescending'. Certainly, a person of nobility would rather die than be the object of Christian pity. If his situation is pitiful he would rather be the object of open and honest disdain. At least that might spur him to improve his situation if at all possible.

Pity is distinct from genuine *compassion*. Pity springs from a sense of duty and/or a condescending sympathy tinged with contempt, dislike and even disgust, while genuine compassion springs from genuine love and is free of negative feelings. Christians claim they love everyone and are therefore capable of genuine compassion for everyone, not just pity. Nietzsche counters that such a generalized love is not really love, that Christian love, as love of all mankind, is phoney and vacuous.

Central to Nietzsche's philosophy, which is really nothing but moral philosophy, is the concept of the *Ubermensch*. The term was abused by Hitler to the extent that it might well evoke in you images of goose-stepping Nazi Stormtroopers, but it simply means *overman*; the man who has overcome himself, the man who has conquered his weaknesses and is the master and creator of his own destiny. It would surely be beneath such a man to be a paid-up fascist or freelance bullyboy. Nietzsche's overman is similar to Aristotle's magnanimous man who, you will recall, fully appreciates that it is vulgar to use one's strength against the weak.

The overman, like the magnanimous man, is more likely to be a philosopher, finding true happiness in a life of quiet contemplation. Nonetheless, if circumstances demand it, he is more than capable of being a brave, resolute and ruthless warrior, of acting decisively without guilt or regret. He is like Colonel Kurtz (Marlon Brando) in the Joseph Conrad and Nietzsche inspired Vietnam War movie *Apocalypse Now* (1979), of whom the American photojournalist (Dennis Hopper) says:

> Hey, man, you don't talk to the Colonel. Well, you listen to him. The man's enlarged my mind. He's a poet-warrior in the classic sense . . . I'm a little man, I'm a little man. He's a great man . . . He can be terrible, and he can be mean, and he can be right . . . You don't judge the colonel like ordinary men.
>
> *Apocalypse Now Redux*, 2001. Director: Francis Ford Coppola. Original screenplay: John Milius and Francis Coppola. All rights reserved © American Zoetrope, 2001. Transcript: Faber & Faber, 2001

Some readers may be tempted to scorn all of this as at best absurd romanticism and at worst highly elitist, and at times even Aristotle sounds like his tongue is somewhat in his cheek as he describes the magnanimous man. But what really is so wrong with much of this stuff, with having proper pride, self-respect and determination, with valuing self-reliance and scorning dependence, with being brave, dignified and tough?

These are actually socially constructive virtues that many people still hold dear and aspire to live by, even if they are virtues that are currently out of fashion in a decadent society that increasingly values and endorses mawkishness, self-pity, vulnerability, victimhood, feeble excuses and sham helplessness over dignity, courage, equanimity, forbearance, self-reliance and self-responsibility.

Would it be so bad if more people aspired instead to emulate, at least to some extent, the proper pride, self-respect and self-discipline of Aristotle's magnanimous man? Aspired to reintroduce at least some of those old, out-of-vogue virtues, like stoicism, or honour, or even nobility and chivalry? How about three cheers for the good old-fashioned stiff upper lip in an age of the constantly quivering lower one?

Then again, perhaps the permanently stiff upper lip no more strikes the golden mean, the golden average, than the constantly quivering lower lip. What is the right balance, the right amount of weeping, for a person with greatness of soul? To weep too often is weakness and vanity, to weep not at all is unfeeling. He or she should weep only on exceptional occasions then, so that their tears are precious and rare. 'From beneath his slouched hat Ahab dropped a tear into the sea; nor did all the Pacific contain such wealth as that one wee drop' (Herman Melville, *Moby-Dick*, p. 590).

Let's calm the waters a little and attempt to see Aristotle's ethics in the broadest terms, in terms that reveal what is most useful about them to anyone, anywhere, regardless of their social standing and so on. Above all, it can be said that Aristotle advocates living life to the maximum by building a well-rounded, balanced existence in which a person does not deprive himself in one area of his reality by overdoing it in another.

Aristotle is a *teleologist*. The words *teleology* and *teleological* derive from the Greek word *telos* which means *end*, *goal* or *purpose*. Aristotle argues that everything in nature has its own *telos*, the true and proper end goal at which it aims, and that we understand what things are by understanding what their end goal is. Teleology is a central principle in various areas of Aristotle's diverse philosophy, including his biology and his ethics.

The *telos* of an acorn, for example, is to become a healthy oak tree producing healthy acorns of its own. For a thing to achieve its *telos*, its end goal, is for it to *flourish*. An acorn that fails to become a healthy oak tree fails to flourish, fails to achieve its *telos*. Its failure to achieve its *telos* is likely to be due to its serving the purposes of another being with its own *telos*. It might, for example, be eaten by a squirrel.

Aristotle seeks to identify the personal virtues that facilitate human flourishing, the virtues that enable a person to forge a full, worthwhile, successful, satisfying life. The most successful life is one that achieves the sustained state of profound happiness and contentment that the ancient Greeks called *eudaimonia*: a fully rounded and balanced life governed by moderation and wisdom. The virtues that facilitate the highest human flourishing of *eudaimonia* accord with what Aristotle calls the *golden mean*.

To strike the golden mean a person must achieve a balance, a happy medium, between various vices of deficiency and excess in the way he approaches his life and other people. If he is too slack or too uptight in the way he lives then his life will be out of tune, in much the same way as a guitar is out of tune if its strings are too tight or too lose.

The virtue of courage, for example, lies between the deficiency of cowardice and the excess of rashness, stupidity or fearlessness. A coward is a person who 'exceeds in fearing' (*Nicomachean Ethics*, 1115b19–1116a6, p. 129). Overwhelmed by his fear, a coward is unable to defend himself or his property or to contribute to the defence of his family and community when enemies who threaten their way of life or very survival must be resisted. A coward will be despised by everyone as a let-down, including himself. Even his enemies will despise him as a man unworthy of respect, if they ever catch sight of him that is.

In fleeing his fear by fleeing what is fearful, a coward is likely to be tormented by shame, although, like Shakespeare's loveable, comical, cowardly knight Sir John Falstaff, who pretends to be dead at the Battle of Shrewsbury to avoid the fight, a coward will often rationalize and misrepresent his cowardly actions to himself and to others in order to render them more palatable. 'The better part of valour is discretion; in the which better part I have saved my life' (*Henry IV, Part One*, Act 5.4, p. 282). Falstaff, of course, is fooling himself. He has no valour for his discretion to be a part of; he simply exercises craven caution.

The rash person, on the other hand, charges into dangerous situations without due consideration. He has not learnt the *true* wisdom of the proverb 'Discretion is the better part of valour' as he always acts without discretion. He is often not such an asset to a cause as he may at first appear to be, as he is likely to get himself and others needlessly injured or killed.

Interestingly, a rash person and a coward are similar, in that neither can bear to feel fear, whereas a courageous person feels fear and bears it. 'The rash man is considered to be both a boaster and a pretender to courage; at any rate he wishes to *seem* as the courageous man really *is* in his attitude towards fearful situations' (*Nicomachean Ethics*, 1115b19–1116a6, p. 129).

A person who, in the category of fear and confidence, strikes the golden mean of courage, faces dangerous situations without hesitation or complaint when it is necessary to defend his own interests and those of his family and community. He is not fearless, only a rash imbecile is fearless in face of earthquakes, infernos or bloody battles. Rather, he controls his fear and refuses to let it master him. In mastering his fear he keeps a clear head and is able to act with resolute purpose, for a prolonged period of time if need be.

His courage is not mere bravado, mere show, although he may sometimes make a show of swaggering before his enemies if that serves the purpose of intimidating them. Strutting his stuff may be enough by itself to cause his enemies to back down. The courageous man does not look for trouble as though he had something to prove. Other virtues, such as modesty, begin to enter the picture here. A person's virtues do not exist in isolation, they tend to enter into one another and support one another.

To take another example, the virtue of generosity lies between the deficiency of meanness and pettiness and the excess of profligacy and extravagance. A stingy person will be disliked, will receive few favours from others and will fail to resource his everyday existence adequately. He will perhaps not feed himself properly or buy cheap, sub-standard tools when he could have afforded tools fit for purpose.

A profligate person who throws his money around, on the other hand, will be exploited by others and will diminish his assets to the extent that he can no longer support himself and his dependants. His displays of extravagance are likely to be viewed as vulgar and foolish rather than genuinely appreciated as generous, not least by those who are keen to take advantage of them for their own gain.

For his part, a person who strikes the golden mean of generosity will be genuinely liked and respected, will find pleasure in pleasing people, will keep enough in reserve to prevent himself and his dependants from becoming a burden on others and will be able to legitimately and successfully call in favours should he ever need to.

Below is a table, similar to Aristotle's own (*Nicomachean Ethics*, 1107b18–20, p. 104), reflecting what he held to be the excess, golden mean and deficiency for a range of actions and feelings:

Area of Action or Feeling	Excess	Golden Mean	Deficiency
Fear and Confidence	Rashness Stupidity Fearlessness	Courage Bravery Valour	Cowardice Gutlessness
Pleasure and Pain	Overindulgence Licentiousness	Moderation Temperance	Insensitivity Dullness
Getting and Spending	Greed Profligacy Extravagance Vulgarity	Generosity Tastefulness	Pettiness Stinginess Meanness
Self-respect	Vanity Arrogance Egotism	Confidence Dignity Proper pride	Servility Submissiveness Humbleness
Anger	Irritability Irascibility	Patience Forbearance	Timidity Passivity

Expressing Yourself	Boastfulness	Truthfulness	Understatement False modesty
Conversation	Buffoonery Ridiculousness	Wittiness	Boorishness Coarseness
Social Conduct	Obsequiousness Creepiness	Friendliness	Tactlessness Rudeness
Shame	Shyness Prissiness	Modesty	Crudeness Obscenity

In introducing Aristotle's ethics to young adult students I have, on many occasions, asked them to produce their own particularly modern virtues and vices table under the heading, 'Virtues for the Twenty First Century: What is the Right Balance?'

Below is one such table I copied from the whiteboard and shoved into my notes after a fun, cool teacher, brainstorming session with the whole class. Deliberately trying to leave things as open as possible for this simple activity, I did not ask students to name the area of action or feeling they had in mind. Some of the responses are dubious, but all are useful food for thought, discussion triggers for further clarification of Aristotle's position. Make of them what you will.

Too Much	The Right Balance	Not Enough
Prostitution	Sex	Celibacy
Size 24	Size 12	Size 6
Bizarre	Creative	Boring
Hyperactive	Mellow	Sluggish
Unnecessary sacrifice	Honour	Selfish action
Creep	Respect for others	Disrespectful
Clown	Sense of humour	Over-serious
'Too cool for school' or 'Only care about your image'	Cool	Sad

Aristotle notes that 'not every action or feeling admits of a mean; because some have names that directly connote depravity' (*Nicomachean Ethics*, 1107a1–27, p. 102). Take *malice*, for example. Malice is not evil in excess or deficiency, malice is evil in itself. Or take theft. 'Theft is theft', we say. 'It is a sin to steal a pin.' In moral terms you cannot have just the right, virtuous amount of theft, with too much theft and not enough theft being vices.

Similar can be said for murder and adultery. 'Nor does acting rightly or wrongly in such cases depend upon circumstances – whether a man commits adultery with the right woman or at the right time or in the right way, because to do anything of that kind is simply wrong' (*Nicomachean Ethics*, 1107a1–27, p. 102).

Is this Aristotle sliding towards a more Kantian view? Not that Kant himself would be around for a couple of millennia yet. Why are theft, murder and adultery 'simply wrong'? Kant would say because they breach the categorical imperative and treat another rational being as a mere means. In the case of adultery, a maxim is willed that if universalized would undermine the convention of marriage and so render adultery, as such, impossible. One cannot rationally endorse both the convention of marriage, vowing to 'forsake all others', and the convention of adultery.

For their part, consequentialists would allow that in some circumstances adultery is morally acceptable, if it relieves a great deal of unhappiness for example, and they would certainly argue that there are cases where theft is morally acceptable. A man stealing bread for his family, for example, when a tyrant has cut off every other means of subsistence.

Aristotle might well argue that it is simply dishonest, dishonourable and undignified for a man to betray his wife, or for a woman to betray her husband, by committing adultery. Not least, the magnanimous man or woman would not wish to characterize themselves in the eyes of society as so lacking in honesty and self-control.

Aristotle says adultery is wrong in itself, but it could perhaps be viewed as wrong because it is a *lack* of fidelity. However, if adultery is the *deficiency* of fidelity, what is the *excess* of fidelity? A person is either faithful to their marriage vows or not. I want to say that a person cannot be *too* faithful, but then we might allow that a wife, for example, who remains perfectly faithful to a husband who beats her and cheats on her is being *excessively* loyal. If this excessive loyalty is a vice then it may be a vice more virtuously addressed by divorce than by adultery.

Importantly, Aristotle recognizes that what constitutes courage, generosity or any other virtue will depend on a person's particular constitution and circumstances. A courageous act for a highly trained special forces commando, for example, may well be a rash and stupid act for a civilian with no military training.

The ancient Greeks inscribed the aphorisms 'Know thyself' and 'Nothing to excess' on the temple of Apollo at Delphi, thought to be the centre of the world, and it was widely understood in their culture that every person must try to use their worldly wisdom and self-knowledge to work out what is the happy medium for them.

Some people can tolerate more alcohol than others, some people have a stronger nerve than others in tense or dangerous situations, some people have a naturally healthy constitution while others do not. Some people are naturally garrulous and have to resist talking too much in order to be polite, others are naturally taciturn and have to make an effort to be sociable in order to be polite. Some people have more money than others such that what is profligacy for one person is generosity for another, and what is generosity for one person is stinginess for another.

If you shook a charity collection box beneath the nose of Jeff Bezos and he popped in just one dollar, you could be forgiven for thinking he was being pretty tight. Although, as more of a credit card kind of guy, maybe one dollar was all the cash he had on him. It is not just about what a person gives but how and why they give it. Perhaps he did not want to appear extravagant, perhaps he already gave at the office, perhaps he really had only one dollar left in the world, having paid his taxes, in which case he was being profligate.

We have all been dealt different hands in life, by chance or by the gods. It is how we play the hand we have been dealt that secures happiness. Aristotle's moral theory is not a rule book, dogmatically saying, you must do this, you must not do that. It is a general philosophical and practical guide to living that invites each individual to honestly and intelligently assess his unique character and situation in order to decide the details of how he should conduct himself in order to achieve the blessing of true happiness.

Aristotle makes practical intelligence, learning from experience, foresight, self-control and proper pride, which together add up to *wisdom*, the basis of moral conduct and goodness. Much that we label wicked is simply the result of gross stupidity, the reckless act of a moment, so much so that it is often the sheer dull-wittedness and self-destructiveness of some acts, even more than their wickedness, that shocks the mind of anyone with two brain cells to rub together.

Only yesterday I heard that a young man had hit a ninety-six-year-old pensioner in the face with a claw hammer, on the pensioner's doorstep, simply because the pensioner declined to have any odd jobs done. There was, apparently, nothing more to the incident than that. Never mind wondering how nasty a person would have to be to do such a thing, the main focus of the media coverage, how much of a moron would a person have to be to do such a thing?

It is said that whatever we do, we do it because it seemed like a good idea at the time, but how on earth could hitting a pensioner in the face with a hammer have seemed like a good idea then or at any time? It served no useful purpose, not even a wicked one. It was a pointless, idiotic, ridiculous, almost totally unprovoked spur-of-the-moment lashing out that is nonetheless likely to ruin the rest of the perpetrator's life (such an idiot is almost certain to be caught – he was) let alone the life of his unfortunate victim.

In many ways, goodness is simply intelligence, especially if we allow that a key aspect of intelligence is self-control. We do not call a person intelligent who seriously lacks self-control. Arguably, the truly intelligent person sees little or no incentive in being anything but good.

Various thinkers, from Socrates to Christopher Marlowe to Henry Ford, have remarked that the only sin or evil is ignorance. Diogenes

Laërtius, not to be confused with the more famous Cynic philosopher Diogenes, who lived in a barrel, quotes Socrates as saying, 'There is only one good, knowledge, and one evil, ignorance' (*Lives of the Eminent Philosophers*, p. 49). Socrates held that if a person truly knows that something is good he will do it. 'No one who either knows or believes that there is another possible course of action, better than the one he is following, will ever continue on his present course when he might choose the better. To 'act beneath yourself' is the result of pure ignorance, to 'be your own master' is wisdom' (Plato, *Protagoras*, 358b–c, p. 95)

So, what of *akrasia*, weakness of will, which we considered earlier? Well, philosophers who agree with Socrates argue that there is really no such thing as akrasia. In considering hammer man's dastardly deed they would say he did not refrain from doing it because he was weak-willed, but because he was ignorant of the fact that not doing the deed was the better option.

If challenged to say which course of action was best, he might well reply, or grunt to the equivalent, 'It is best not to hit people in the face with a hammer, unless acting in self-defence.' However, so the argument goes, he does not really *understand* that it is best, does not really *believe* that it is best, has never really taken on board the sound advice that violence rarely pays, that violence is usually a bad way, and always a desperate way, of dealing with other people. In his ignorance, he somehow believed striking the blow was best, which is why he did it.

This is a huge topic that I am only able to touch upon here, but certainly the philosophical jury is still out as to whether there is genuine akrasia, or merely what may look like akrasia but is actually only ignorance.

Finally, not least to get away from the depressing thought of hammer-wielding cretins, it is worth taking a brief look at the central Buddhist concept of the *middle way*, which is remarkably similar to the Aristotelian notion of the golden mean. So much so that it is a wonder we do not also have little plump statues of Aristotle all around our homes and gardens alongside the many we already have of the Buddha.

Most scholars now place the death of Gautama Buddha within twenty years either side of 400 BCE. Aristotle was born in 384 BCE. Remarkably close in time given the vast history of philosophy. Although there is no evidence that Aristotle knew of Gautama Buddha's teachings directly, Eastern thought was known in the ancient Greek world. Both men were undoubtedly influenced by the same *zeitgeist*, and to some extent codified and developed various ideas that were circulating on the ancient trade routes.

Recall our example from earlier of the out-of-tune guitar. It is actually Buddha who compares a person to a musical instrument and his life to the tune he plays. To follow the middle way is to strive for *attunement*: a bringing into harmony, concord, balance and unity. Prince Siddhartha, who became Gautama Buddha, is supposed to have once heard a musician say to his pupil, 'If you tighten the strings too much they will snap, if they are too loose they will not play', and the rest, as they say, is history.

Within Buddhism the middle way has been significantly widened, like an upgraded section of the eternal circle of the M25, to become the *noble eightfold path*. Learn to walk these eight often intertwining paths simultaneously, such that doing so becomes second nature to you, and you will be liberated from the suffering you bring upon yourself through your wrong attitudes and actions. Very briefly the eightfold path is:

1 *Right understanding*: Seeing life as it really is rather than as you want it to be.

2 *Right intent*: Heartfelt commitment to following the path.

3 *Right speech*: Be careful what you say and how you say it. Words are deeds.

4 *Right action*: Ethical conduct. Treat others and the world with respect.

5 *Right livelihood*: Find socially constructive employment, avoid socially destructive employment.

6 *Right effort*: Enthusiasm for all you do but not too slow and not too hasty.

7 *Right mindfulness*: Be aware of the present moment, not constantly distracted.

8 *Right concentration*: Full, calming focus on objects and concepts. Basic meditation. More advanced meditation dispenses with objects and concepts.

Returning from the mystic East, recall that Aristotle also believes that contemplation is essential for true happiness. Both Buddhism and Aristotelianism have an important spiritual element as well as being practical guides to everyday living. Indeed, a major step towards the good life, goodness, happiness, *eudaimonia*, enlightenment is realizing that the practical life and the spiritual life are really one and the same and therefore should not be separated.

Goodness and Freedom

As we saw earlier in this book, the existentialist philosopher Jean-Paul Sartre holds that we cannot not be free. He put the point well when he said that we are 'condemned to be free' (*Being and Nothingness*, p. 462). This is probably the second most famous thing he ever said after 'Hell is other people' (*In Camera*, p. 223).

To go through life is to be constantly confronted by the inescapability of having to choose. You might think, well, sometimes I can duck a choice between A and B by sitting on the fence, by not choosing. Well, you may duck A and B by doing this but you have not ducked *choosing* because you have chosen C: sitting on the fence. As Sartre puts it, 'Not to choose is, in fact, to choose not to choose' (*Being and Nothingness*, p. 503).

Lots of people, including me in other books, like to bang on about existentialism being this wonderful philosophy of radical *freedom*, and certainly it is, but what is less trumpeted, because less attractive and more irksome, is that it is also a philosophy of radical *responsibility*. To be condemned to be free is to bear the constant responsibility of having to choose a path, or a fence to sit on, and to be constantly responsible for whatever path or fence is chosen.

We are all shaped to some extent by our context, the time and place we were born, our upbringing, our friends and so on. But once we move beyond infancy we are also hugely shaped by the choices we make in *response* to that context. As we are not fixed things like stones or chairs, but rather indeterminate beings in constant process of becoming and change, our choices shape who we are. We are, in many ways, the product of our choices.

Teachers, fellow students, the whole school experience, for example, may be somewhat responsible for a person's life situation now. However, the effect of a person's school years on his adult life, positive and negative, probably had far more to do with the myriad choices *he* made while he was at school and is therefore responsible for. Many people do not like to hear this as it suggests that school is not really such a convenient *scapegoat* for their underachievement as they like to think. It is a fair response to many adults who complain about their lot, particularly in developed countries, that they should have tried harder at school.

At one time I wanted to be a scientist. Perversely, however, I failed science at school because I chose to sit by class clowns in every science lesson and to lark about with them at every opportunity rather than focus on Hooke's Law or photosynthesis. Nobody made me sit by the jokers and time-wasters and my teachers would have been relieved had I moved desks. Admittedly, it would have been un-cool to move desks but it was still my choice to sit where I sat and to misbehave as I did.

I do not regret fooling about in science lessons at school because I do not regret not having become a scientist. Not least, it was such priceless high jinks that it was worth failing for, although, I now recognize, it selfishly disrupted those students who wanted to pass.

The point is, however, if I did regret not having become a scientist, and tried to blame my failure on my hard-pressed teachers or the tatty but just about adequate resources they had at their disposal, I would be in *bad faith*.

Bad faith is seeking to evade responsibility. Bad faith is blaming other people and circumstances for the choices you made and for the consequences of those choices. Bad faith is acting as though you did not or do not have a choice. Often, bad faith is treating yourself as though you are a *thing*, an object acted upon, rather than a being that acts upon the world in accordance with its choices; a being that shapes the world and itself through its choices and actions.

We are all motivated to some extent to pretend to ourselves and others that we are things. That huge, unending burden of freedom and responsibility makes us *anxious*, makes us want simply to *be* who were are, rather than have to constantly *choose* who we are without ever being able to finally be at one with ourselves.

In *Being and Nothingness*, Sartre illustrates the anxiety of freedom and responsibility through the example of *vertigo*, as did Søren Kierkegaard before him in his book *The Concept of Anxiety* (1844). 'Anxiety,' said Kierkegaard, 'is the dizziness of freedom' (*The Concept of Anxiety*, p. 61). In analysing vertigo both thinkers make an important distinction between fear and anxiety. A person *fears* that he might accidentally fall or be pushed off a precipice or high building. On the other hand, he is *anxious* that he is free to jump and that there is nothing to stop him from jumping except his own free choice not to do so, a free choice that must be constantly renewed and might not be renewed. That woozy, anxious feeling of vertigo is concern that at any moment he could, and just might, *decide* to jump.

It is better, then, as a means of reducing both the risk he poses to himself and his anxiety about that risk, for him to try and convince himself, in bad faith, that he is just not the sort of person-*thing* that could ever decide to jump. That it is just not in him, that he is just too sensible, too timid, that his survival instincts are just too strong and so on.

Existentialists tend to see bad faith as a very bad thing. Not only is it a denial of our true nature, something that we need to overcome if we are to achieve our full potential as free human beings, they see it as an attitude that, if not evil in itself, easily lends itself to the purposes of evil. Recall Eichmann's contemptible display of bad faith, his insistence that in helping to perpetrate the Holocaust he was only following orders, that he had no choice but to act as he did.

In the case of the person susceptible to vertigo, however, bad faith appears to be a good thing, a way of reducing anxiety, a coping strategy. It protects the psychological well-being of a person by serving as a guard rail against anxiety. This in turn is good for a person's physical well-being because anxiety, as a form of stress, is unhealthy. Bad faith also directly protects the physical well-being of a person by serving as a guard rail against dangerous experiments in the exercise of freedom.

Having said all this, it has to be acknowledged that Eichmann too was using bad faith as a stress-reducing coping strategy, as a guard rail against the shame and self-loathing he might have suffered had he at least the decency, the honesty, the courage to take even the smallest amount of personal responsibility for his actions. Bad faith is a convenient barrier for cowards to hide behind.

Some people might even feel that Eichmann's banal, irresponsible, cowardly brand of evil was somehow even more abhorrent than that of honest Nazis who took full, proud responsibility for their actions without regret. Perhaps because Eichmann's indifferent hand-rinsing failed to give his victims what was due to them: his recognition that they were indeed his victims. While awaiting trial Eichmann said, 'To sum it all up, I must say that I regret nothing' (*Life Magazine*, 5 December 1960), but this was only because he believed he was not responsible for anything. This is very different from taking full responsibility for something and not regretting it.

A more mundane example of bad faith functioning as a bad thing is its role in sustaining debilitating phobias. Arguably, a phobia can be conquered by overcoming the bad faith within which it functions.

Achieving an intellectual awareness of bad faith can be the first step towards a person conquering his claustrophobia, for example. Realizing that he cannot be a person who fears confined spaces in the mode of being a fearing *thing*, he will realize that he must be choosing himself, in bad faith, as a person who has no choice but to fear confined spaces; a choice that he reaffirms every time he acts fearfully towards a confined space.

The solution to the phobia is for him to refrain by an act of will from all behaviour that re-enforces his false belief that his fear is a thing; a possession that determines his responses. Eventually, he will expose his fear as nothing but a self-perpetuating project of fear that he has abandoned by changing his behaviour.

That it would be advantageous for a person to overcome certain projects of bad faith does not imply that it would be advantageous for him to overcome bad faith completely. Particular disadvantages of bad faith must be weighed against overall advantages. A person who, for example, is hampered and repressed in some respects by neuroses maintained in bad faith would not necessarily gain by overcoming these neuroses.

His neurotic behaviour might be a more or less harmless means of dissipating anxiety that would otherwise cause him a mental breakdown. In this case, as in the case of the vertigo sufferer, bad faith can be seen as a useful coping strategy. Neurotic behaviour maintained in bad faith might even be the key to a person's success if it disposes him towards organization in his life and perfectionism in his work.

So, sometimes bad faith can be very dangerous and damaging, at other times harmless and helpful. Arguably, bad faith is not really morally good or bad in itself, even though it is essentially an attitude of dishonesty. Bad faith cuts both ways. Like a knife it can have morally good or morally bad consequences depending on who possesses it and how and when and for what reason it is exercised. This can be described as a broadly utilitarian perspective on bad faith.

However, if we think of goodness from an Aristotelian perspective, as being about a person achieving his *telos*, achieving his full potential as a human being, then bad faith is surely a vice, precisely because a person in bad faith is a person failing to achieve his full potential. In so far as being in bad faith is a person pretending to himself that he is not free, responsible and indeterminate then it is him denying and stifling his true nature.

It will be objected that if we are fundamentally free, responsible and indeterminate then it is impossible for us ever to be other than that. Well, it is impossible for us ever to be other than that but importantly bad faith is using what we are against ourselves. As choosing not to choose, as choosing to pretend that we have no choice, bad faith is the exercise of our inalienable freedom to deny and repress our freedom. Bad faith is freedom exercised against itself, exercised negatively. It is *negative freedom*.

We are also capable, however, of *positive freedom*, of exercising our freedom positively, constructively, expressively, non-repressively, honestly and responsibly, to create ourselves and shape a unique destiny for ourselves. This positive freedom is called *authenticity*, and is the holy grail of existentialism. Authenticity is the overcoming of bad faith. To be in bad faith is to be *inauthentic*. Authenticity may not be the key to happiness – existentialists are not big on happiness, they tend to associate it with bovine contentment – but only in striving for authenticity can we hope to become fully realized, fully actualized, fully functioning human beings.

The distinction between positive freedom and negative freedom is akin to Nietzsche's distinction between slave-morality and master-morality that we considered earlier. Negative freedom, freedom that denies, checks and represses itself, is an aspect of what Nietzsche calls the *ascetic ideal*, the valuing of self-repression over self-expression that lies at the heart of *slave-morality*. Positive freedom, on the other hand, the positive affirmation of freedom, is an aspect of what Nietzsche calls the *noble ideal*, the valuing of self-expression over self-repression that lies at the heart of *master-morality*.

A noble or authentic person positively affirms himself as a free being. He does not deny and repress his freedom but enjoys it and is constantly aware of it. He does this by acting decisively, overcoming difficulties, self-actualizing, living life to the full, taking full responsibility for his past deeds and his present circumstances and refusing to regret.

When the going gets tough, rather than wish he was someone else somewhere else, an authentic person accepts what Sartre calls his *being-in-situation*. Rather than complaining about his situation, or even allowing himself to be unduly surprised by it, he immediately embraces it, looks at it honestly and realistically and tackles it head on, dealing with it and making the most of it. Like the magnanimous man, or the overman, the authentic person is always ready for whatever life throws at him. A true warrior, a true hero, he does not invite trouble but he is always ready for it. He knows that in life one should always expect the unexpected. In his *War Diaries* (1939–40), Sartre says:

> To be authentic is to realise fully one's being-in-situation, whatever this situation may happen to be: with a profound awareness that, through the authentic realisation of the being-in-situation, one brings to plenary existence the situation on the one hand and human reality on the other. This presupposes a patient study of what the situation requires, and then a way of throwing oneself into it and determining oneself to 'be-for' this situation.
>
> *War Diaries*, p. 54

Sartre goes as far as to say that even if a person has not chosen to be in the situation in which he finds himself, he should nonetheless immediately take ownership of the situation as though he had chosen it. When called to fight in World War II, for example, rather than grumble about the interruption to his pleasant civilian life, Sartre undertook to *choose* the war. He firmly decided that he was not in a situation that was merely happening *to* him. Choosing his past, even his birth, he determined that his life had all been leading to that time and place. He took full possession of his situation without regret.

As to regret, like Nietzsche before him, Sartre recognizes that a person who regrets is inauthentic. A person who regrets wishes he had acted differently in the past, he wishes his past were different. As a person *is* his past, the sum total of all the choices he has made, to regret his past is to wish that he were not the person he is. Authenticity, as the positive affirmation of freedom, requires that a person take full responsibility for *all* his choices, not only those he is making and will make, but all those he has made in the past. Only by taking full responsibility for all his choices, past, present and future does a person take full responsibility for who he is.

It can be argued that a person who regrets takes responsibility for his past, in so far as to regret past deeds is to acknowledge them. Regret, however, is a wholly negative and irresponsible acknowledgement. It acknowledges only to renounce and disavow. A person who regrets does not say, 'Yes, I did that deed and it is now a part of who I am', he says, 'I wish I had not done that deed, that it was not a part of who I am'. As we all know, to regret is to dwell uselessly on the past wishing the past were different.

To cease to regret is to change the meaning of the past by choosing and affirming the past. The authentic person always seeks to define past events positively as he moves towards the future. He treats them as a learning experience, or as an experience that made him stronger or wiser, or he strives to render them positive by giving them a positive outcome. It is important to recognize that a person's ongoing actions define the meaning of his past. A man who quits his job, for example, can come to regret it or by his ongoing efforts define his resignation as a positive step.

Nietzsche argues that the ideal way to live is to dispense with regret so thoroughly, to love your past, your entire life, so completely, that you want each and every moment of your existence to recur eternally. Nietzsche calls this his *formula for greatness*. 'My formula for greatness for a human being is *amor fati* [love fate]: that one wants nothing to be other than it is, not in the future, not in the past, not in all eternity' (*Ecce Homo*: *How one Becomes What One Is*, p. 68). This is certainly a tall order, but Nietzsche's uncompromising thought is that if you do not want to live your life over again in every detail then you are not living it right. And if you do not want your life over again in every detail, then do you really want it now?

If authenticity involves living without regret, then it can be argued that authenticity is impossible because it is impossible to live without regret. Regret, it seems, is an unavoidable feature of the human condition because anyone with the capacity to imagine alternatives cannot help wishing, at least occasionally, that they had made a different decision.

In response to this objection it can be argued that it does not show authenticity is impossible, simply that it is very difficult to achieve. If a person can come to regret less then arguably he has the potential to master himself completely and regret nothing.

Perhaps the task of complete self-mastery and self-overcoming is too difficult to achieve in one lifetime, particularly for people raised in a culture of regret and recrimination. Yet it remains a noble ideal worth striving for because it is surely always better to take charge of one's life and one's situation than it is to be what Sartre calls a *buffeted consciousness*, a consciousness that sees itself as a given or fixed entity buffeted and swept along by circumstances.

It is better, not least, because a person who constantly strives to confront his situation and overcome it, a person who thereby constantly strives to confront and overcome himself, gains self-respect. A cowardly person, on the other hand, who dwells on regret, refusing to confront his situation and his being in that situation, knows only his own weakness and sense of defeat. Anyone might slip into regret at any moment. What Sartre wants to stress is that everyone is capable of overcoming regret by exercising their freedom positively and thereby taking responsibility for their past.

A person can clearly construct a personal ethics out of striving for authenticity, one that gives the highest value to one's own dignity, integrity and courage, but can authenticity also be the basis of an ethical code proper, an ethical code concerned with how people ought to treat each other? Well, as we have seen, authenticity is all about confronting life for what it is, all about being-in-situation. It is all about accepting and affirming the fundamental, inescapable existential truths of the human condition. Not only those we have already focused on: freedom, responsibility and indeterminacy, but also *mortality*, *desire*, *contingency* (that existence is not necessary), *being-for-others* (that we exist for other people) and, last but by no means least, certainly as far as answering the above ethical question is concerned, *the freedom of others*.

As the freedom of others is one of the fundamental, inescapable truths of the human condition then it follows that it is *authentic* to acknowledge, accept and affirm the freedom of others. That is, it is *inauthentic* to ignore and disrespect in other people what one recognizes so acutely and values so highly in oneself. This view, this basis for an existentialist ethics, is at least suggested in Sartre's *Notebooks for an Ethics* (1945–8).

At the end of *Being and Nothingness* Sartre wrote that he would consider the ethical implications of his theory of the human condition in a later work. That he seriously intended to produce a fully developed existentialist ethics is revealed by the extensive notes he made on ethics between 1945 and 1948, nearly 600 pages of which were published posthumously in 1983 as *Notebooks for an Ethics*.

These working notes show Sartre musing, brainstorming, thinking against himself and developing his thoughts. In places, he may not even agree with what he has written down. Having said this, there is sufficient consistency and recurrence of themes in the notebooks for some general conclusions to be drawn. Some ideas expressed can also be checked against ideas found in published works written around the same time, such as Sartre's *Existentialism and Humanism* (1946) and de Beauvoir's *The Ethics of Ambiguity* (1947). Sartre and de Beauvoir collaborated very closely during this period, holding many ideas in common.

Although the notebooks offer interesting insights into the possible nature of an ethics consistent with Sartre's theory of human reality, they do not succeed in detailing such an ethics. A synthesis between existentialism and ethics is not achieved and may be ultimately unachievable. The notebooks do not answer the question of what ethics *is* for Sartre, they show Sartre in the process of trying to decide that question for himself. The notebooks are a process of enquiry that Sartre hoped would eventually allow him to write a book presenting a fully worked-out existentialist ethics.

Unfortunately, due to other commitments and perhaps the impossibility of the task, he never wrote such a book. As he wrote elsewhere, 'Published after my death, these texts will remain unfinished and obscure, since they formulate ideas which are not completely developed. It will be up to the reader to decide where they might have led' (*Life/Situations*, pp. 74–5).

What is certainly clear is Sartre's view that an existentialist ethics cannot be based on an abstract, *a priori* moral principle such as Kant's categorical imperative. It is this view that prevents Sartre from aligning his position with that of Kant, even though he is repeatedly tempted towards a broadly Kantian position in other respects, as he is in various areas of his philosophy.

Sartre also rejects, as he does in *Existentialism and Humanism*, an ethics based on the existence of a moral God. Like Nietzsche and de Beauvoir, Sartre is an atheist who argues that the existence of God is impossible. He argues that we are *abandoned* in an essentially meaningless universe with no God to give us purpose or moral direction.

What is also clear is that Sartre sees ethics as an other-person-related phenomenon, as a feature of our *being-for-others*. This position is consistent with what has already been said in this book, that moral goodness and moral badness are largely to do with how people treat each other. Sartre argues that no action is unethical until another person judges it to be so.

An ethical state of affairs, although Sartre does not say how it is to be achieved, is one in which people respect and affirm each other's freedom. His difficulty is to accommodate this claim with his view that the freedom of other people inevitably negates and cancels out my freedom. Other people only have to look at me, be conscious of me and judge me to reduce me from being the centre of my world to being an object in their world.

Sartre says the consciousness of the Other inevitably *transcends* mine, reducing me to what he calls a *transcendence-transcended*. As I am Other to the Other I can also, in turn, transcend his consciousness. And so on it goes, endlessly back and forth. Hence, Sartre argues in *Being and Nothingness* that 'The essence of the relations between consciousnesses is not the *Mitsein* [being-with-others]; it is conflict' (*Being and Nothingness*, p. 451). In short, 'Hell is other people' (*In Camera*, p. 223).

Sartre takes the position that the objectification and alienation of a person by others, although unavoidable on a mundane level, need not result in active oppression as it has done historically. Although people will always experience themselves as objects for others, they need never be *mere* objects for others.

A person is capable of recognizing on all occasions that the human object before him is also a person and a free transcendent consciousness; what Sartre's contemporary Maurice Merleau-Ponty in his book *The Phenomenology of Perception* (1945) refers to as an *embodied consciousness*. For Sartre, to recognize and affirm one's own freedom is to be *authentic*, while to respect and affirm the freedom of others is to be *ethical*.

It appears to follow from this that a person must be authentic to be ethical, he must affirm his own freedom in order to affirm the freedom of others. That is, he must fully recognize freedom in himself in order to achieve full recognition of freedom in others. In short, a person must be authentic to affirm the freedom of others.

As said, to be authentic is to recognize and embrace the fundamental, inescapable existential truths of the human condition, one of these existential truths being the inexorable existence of the freedom of others. Therefore, not only must a person be authentic to affirm the existential truth of the freedom of others, to affirm the freedom of others *is* to be authentic. Arguably, ethics is other-related authenticity.

Seemingly, an existentially ethical world would be one where a history driven by human freedom has realized an end to the exploitation and oppression that results when one freedom does not respect and affirm another. For Sartre, how this world is to be achieved is unclear. For Kant, as we have seen, it is to be achieved by every person adhering unerringly to the universal moral principle of the categorical imperative. Sartre, however, will not help himself to the categorical imperative because, as a down-to-earth existentialist opposed to anything even vaguely metaphysical, he refuses to base his ethics on *a priori* moral principles.

For Sartre, it appears that behaving ethically is a matter of acting authentically in any given, concrete situation involving others, rather than a matter of stubbornly adhering to the same abstract universal principle in each and every situation involving others. Sartre's ideal ethical world is surely very similar to Kant's kingdom of ends, a world in which every person treats every other person as a free, rational, self-determining end-in-himself, rather than as a mere means lacking freedom; a mere depersonalized object acted upon. In advocating something similar to Kant's kingdom of ends Sartre's ethics is undeniably somewhat Kantian.

Somewhat Hegelian too, given that, as we have seen, Hegel's position here is also rather Kantian. Considering the relationship between history and ethics, Sartre agrees with Hegel that as we do not presently have a world where every free, rational being fully respects and affirms every other free, rational being then this ethical utopia can only be achieved, if it is at all achievable, via an historical process that morally perfects people through the perfection of their political and social institutions. Not surprisingly, Sartre became a disciple of Hegel's revolutionary student Karl Marx.

In wanting to make his ethics a matter of authentic responses to concrete situations, however, responses that depend on the authentic assessment of situations rather than upon an adherence to a universal moral principle, Sartre is not a Kantian deontologist but arguably the advocate of a form of virtue ethics. Somewhat like the virtue ethics of Aristotle, Sartre's ethics is not about dutifully following rigid, abstract moral rules, but about achieving one's full potential and flourishing as a free, responsible human being alongside other free, responsible human beings.

3
THE REALITY OF GOODNESS

Meta-ethics

I have mentioned two or three times already that moral philosophy is not just about trying to work out what goodness and badness or rightness and wrongness are, but about trying to work out if these 'things' are *real* or not. In taking on that task, two key questions immediately arise: If they are real, in what sense are they real? If they are not real, what is ethics really?

This may all sound rather obscure and abstract and in some ways it certainly is. In our non-abstract, everyday lives we are very familiar with people trying to decide what is right and what is wrong, what is good and what is bad, but not at all familiar with people trying to decide if there is any such thing as right and wrong or if good and bad really exist. Recall solipsism. We are very familiar with people trying to decide *what* a person is thinking, but not at all familiar, unless you happen to be a philosopher, with trying to decide whether or not any person besides yourself has a mind in the first place.

The area of moral philosophy that deals with questions of reality and meaning in ethics has the grand-sounding title *meta-ethics*. It sounds like the name of a grand ethical code for people who want to be especially good, but it is not that at all.

Meta means 'of a higher or second-order kind', and it is often said that meta-ethics deals with *second-order* questions in ethics. Normative ethics, meanwhile, deals with the kind of *first-order* questions in ethics about the right things to do and the right ways to live that formed the bulk of the previous chapter. Roughly, meta-ethics is asking and trying to answer questions *about* ethical questions. In his excellent book *Contemporary Metaethics* (2003) Alexander Miller says:

> Suppose I am debating with a friend the question whether or not we ought to give to famine relief, whether or not we are morally obliged to give to famine relief. The sorts of questions philosophers raise about this kind of debate fall roughly into two groups. First, there are *first-order* questions about which party in the debate, if any, is right, and why. Then, there are *second-order* questions about what the parties in the debate are doing when they engage in it.
>
> *Contemporary Metaethics*, p. 1

The central debate in meta-ethics concerns the *objectivity* of ethics. Can moral judgements really be true or false or is there really no moral truth or moral falsehood to be found? Is ethics actually all *subjective*, a matter of feelings rather than facts? In short, are there moral facts?

Moral philosophers divide into two distinct camps depending on the answers they give to these questions. One camp endorses *moral objectivism*, also known as *moral realism* or *cognitivism*, while the other camp endorses *moral subjectivism*, also known as *moral anti-realism* or *non-cognitivism*. Let us visit each camp in turn and rummage around their tents.

Moral Objectivism

If something is objective it is real in some way. To be real it does not have to be physical, simply independent of our thoughts, inclinations and desires, certainly in the sense of not being whatever we want it to be. Consider maths for example. Maths is abstract and conceptual rather than physical but it is nonetheless objective and real because the values, relationships and truths that comprise maths are independent of our subjective whims. $2 + 2 = 4$ whether we like it or not.

A normative moral theory is held to be objective if what the theory stipulates in terms of behaviour is governed by rules, principles and goals that are independent of personal desires and inclinations. Personal inclinations and desires may or may not be in accordance with what the theory stipulates but certainly the theory cannot be influenced by them. 'Do what you like' and 'I will do what I like' are not really rules.

The English occultist, poet and mountaineer Aleister Crowley famously said, 'Do what thou wilt shall be the whole of the law' (*The Book of the Law*, p. 13). If that is the whole of the law, however, then there is no law. Crowley is said to have derived his principle from earlier utterances of 'Do what thou wilt', some of which include a qualification along the lines of 'as long as ye harm none'. Also, his famous line, at least in the place quoted, is directly followed by the line, 'Love is the law, love under will.' These qualifications, which remind us of Mill's *harm principle* considered earlier, make all the difference between a mere expression of selfishness and a moral rule.

A normative moral theory is objective if a person cannot be released from its requirements simply because he desires to act contrary to its requirements. As Miller says, 'I cannot release myself from the requirement imposed by the claim that torturing the innocent is wrong by citing some desire or inclination that I have' (*Contemporary Metaethics*, p. 108).

Moral objectivists may disagree as to which moral theories are genuinely objective, but they all agree that moral objectivity is possible somehow. Mill and Kant, for example, both think that there are objective grounds for distinguishing right from wrong, they just disagree about the grounds. Mill, as we have seen, argues that you cannot base a coherent moral theory on abstract, purely rational, *a priori* principles, while Kant, as we have seen, argues that you cannot base a coherent moral theory on an empirical assessment of the consequences of actions.

Religion is moral objectivism in its oldest and most basic form. Religion insists that there are moral facts, and that the facts are the facts because God said so. Nothing can appear to be more objective, more real in the crudest sense of *real*, than a God-given moral code literally set in stone by God or delivered in person by divine messengers. Religion is largely about following, without question, the commandments of religious authorities and holy books.

Religious people, at least those fundamentalists who feel compelled to visit your front door, will seek to answer all questions you put to them, including moral ones, by referring to their holy book, not thinking, not daring to think, that the holy book itself can be questioned.

If adherents to a religious moral code are tempted to question the code at all, they tend to quickly conclude that *God knows why* these rules, and not other rules, are the rules; that *God knows what* the true objective basis of it all really is, even if they do not. They declare that it is not for the sheep to question the shepherd, and conveniently, the blind trust and faith they are encouraged to have, as opposed to a leaning towards independent thought, means that they do not have to question the shepherd.

Of course, if adherents to a religious moral code *seriously* questioned the code then they would soon be troubling their priests to tell them *why* God says certain actions and feelings are good and others bad. They would soon be demanding an answer to the age old question, 'Is what is good loved by God because it is good, or is it good because it is loved by God?' In short, they would inevitably hit upon Plato's Euthyphro question.

Even if the existence of God was proved beyond all doubt, the Euthyphro question would still reveal that ethics based on religion is not necessarily objectively sound. Legitimate questions could still be raised regarding the principles governing God's moral rules, questions as to why God has certain moral rules and not others.

If God, his existence proved, deigned to answer these questions, he might disclose that other principles are at work besides his *subjective* say-so, thus finally revealing that religious morality is not based on arbitrary divine will after all, but upon, for example, the categorical imperative.

Religious morality, of course, is highly unlikely to be the word of God. It is far more likely to be the word of a ruling class that, at least in the past, wanted those they ruled to follow certain rules. Perhaps scaring the lower ranks into following these rules benefited the ruling class, perhaps the ruling class imposing these rules was the best way to avoid anarchy, perhaps both. Whatever the reason, there was arguably no better way at the time to make people obey moral rules than to brainwash and frighten them into thinking that the rules were the commandments of a divine being who would punish them, perhaps for all eternity, if they disobeyed.

Putting the fear of God into people is no longer one of the main ways in which the ruling classes maintain their power and the general social order. Since the Enlightenment and the rise of science and mass education, too many people have become sceptics, agnostics or even outright atheists for the 'fear of God ploy' to any longer work effectively as a primary method of social control. Commenting on the consequences of the Enlightenment for the feasibility of the idea of God as an explanation for nature and morality, Nietzsche says, 'God is dead. God remains dead. And we have killed him' (*The Gay Science*, 125, p. 181).

Nonetheless, many people in the world today are still religious and follow religious moral codes out of fear, devotion or mere unthinking habit. Many of the rest follow the *residues* of these codes, partly as a result of upbringing and habit, partly because they see them as broadly sensible in themselves regardless of the dubious metaphysics that supposedly underpins them.

Arguably, one could follow the moral teachings of Jesus, for example, without believing any of the metaphysics: son of God, miracles, resurrection, eternal reward and so on. This suggests that non-religious reasons can be found for following many moral rules that were once thought of as objective *because* they were thought of as dictated by God.

A philosopher who is very much a moral objectivist is Plato. Plato argues in *The Republic* and other dialogues that the physical world, the world we encounter through our senses, is a mere appearance, a mere shadow cast by the higher reality of perfect, eternal, metaphysical *forms*.

Forms are not accessible to the senses, only to the mind. The form of squareness, for example, is the *idea* of the perfect square. Only this universal idea is truly real, unlike particular square things in the physical world that lack being perfectly square and are only recognized as more or less square by the degree to which they approximate to the form of perfect squareness.

Forms, argues Plato, are arranged in a hierarchy, with forms of shapes and physical objects, like squares and chairs, lower down, and forms of concepts, like courage and justice, higher up. Particular acts of courage and particular instances of justice participate in or reflect the perfect form to which they correspond. The highest form is the form of *the Good*. The Good is the source of all reality and knowledge, including moral knowledge.

Plato compares the Good to the sun (*The Republic*, 507a, p. 231). Just as the sun is the source of all growth and seeing in the physical world, so the Good is the source of all being and knowledge in the metaphysical world, of which, as said, the physical world is merely a shadow.

Plato's idea of the Good is similar to the Judeo-Christian idea of God – timeless, uncaused, perfect, that from which all else flows – although Plato does not conceive of the Good as personal. 'Christianity is Platonism for "the people"' (Nietzsche, *Beyond Good and Evil*, p. 32). So, for Plato, *goodness* literally exists as an actual objective entity. Indeed, as the highest and most real objective entity from which all other entities, all natural and moral phenomena, derive.

So, a guide to Platonic goodness might well be a large Ordnance Survey map with a fat black arrow drawn on it in permanent marker pointing to the top of the pyramid of forms, an arrow indicating 'The Good lies this way'. The difficulty, however, is getting all the way there, as the Good itself lies off the edge of any map. Plato recognizes that it is impossible to say exactly what the Good is. Even he can only hint at its nature through similes and metaphors.

If you ever achieve a vision of the Good, however, you will be in no doubt that you have arrived because the Good is by definition beyond all doubt. It is a place, a state, of perfect knowledge. In another sense, as the source of all reality, the Good must be everywhere, in all things. The great philosophical, meditative and moral challenge is learning to recognize it.

Plato equates virtue with wisdom. The truly wise person sees beyond the misleading appearances of the physical world about which only opinions and beliefs are possible. He has *knowledge* of the eternal forms and, above all, an understanding of the Good. He is no longer tempted by the things of the physical world as he knows they are fleeting, illusory and more or less worthless.

In no longer being subject to earthly desires the truly wise person cannot be corrupted through them. Beyond the bare essentials, Plato's truly wise person needs earthly goodies like a fish needs a bicycle. Having true knowledge of the timeless and unchanging forms, as opposed to mere opinions and beliefs about an inconstant physical world of mere appearances, he has thoroughly sound judgement.

As an incorruptible person of thoroughly sound judgement he should be in charge of society. He does not want to be in charge, he would rather spend his life contemplating the forms, but he dutifully takes charge to prevent those less able from doing so, that is, eager, self-serving politicians with poor judgement.

Plato wisely argues that those who want to rule should never be allowed to do so because desire for power is the road to corruption, and corrupt power is just about the worst evil that can befall a society. 'The state whose prospective rulers come to their duties with least enthusiasm is bound to have the best and most tranquil government, and the state whose rulers are eager to rule the worst' (*The Republic*, 520d, p. 247).

Plato is famous for arguing that only philosophers should be kings, as only they have the knowledge, skill and integrity to rule well. 'The troubles of mankind will never cease until either true and genuine philosophers attain political power or the rulers of states by some dispensation of providence become genuine philosophers' (Plato, *Seventh Letter*, p. 114). The just society, the one that reflects most clearly the metaphysical form of justice, is a society led by philosopher kings.

As most people are not up to being philosopher kings, and most people do not need to be philosopher kings, the rest of the population, soldiers, workers and so on, should willingly obey their wise, unselfish philosopher rulers. They should live moderately, focus on doing their own designated tasks to perfection and, above all, not interfere in the tasks of others, particularly the highly important and highly skilled task of governance. Hence, Plato despises democracy as the rule of the mob. And so we find ourselves back at Plato's definition of justice as *minding one's own business* (*The Republic*, 434c, p. 139).

For a moral theory to at the very least claim that it is *objective* it must lay claim to some objectifying factor, principle or goal (objective); some *non-subjective* outward criteria that gives it a foothold in a world, a reality, beyond the realm of mere personal, shifting, vacillating feelings, whims and inclinations. Or to put it another way, moral distinctions must be made in accordance with objective rules that are, or could be, publicly intelligible. A private morality in which moral distinctions are made in accordance with a person's wishes and urges is unintelligible as a morality because the 'rules' of this private morality, being arbitrary and inconsistent, are unrecognizable as rules.

As we have seen, for religious moral codes the objectifying factor is divine authority. For Plato, it is knowing the form of the Good and/or minding one's own business within a just society. For Kant, it is reason and logic centring upon the categorical imperative. For Mill, it is the greatest happiness principle, involving the maximization of pleasure and the minimization of pain. For Aristotle, it is striking the golden mean and achieving *eudaimonia*. For Buddha, it is finding the middle way and achieving enlightenment. For Sartre, it is overcoming bad faith and striving for authenticity. These factors, principles and goals are not necessarily mutually exclusive. We have already explored the extent to which some overlap others, as well as the extent to which some conflict with others.

Although some moral objectivists, Kant for example, are moral *absolutists*, believing that certain actions are always *intrinsically* right or wrong regardless of context or consequences, moral objectivism does not necessarily imply moral absolutism. It is possible to be a moral objectivist while maintaining that 'Circumstances alter cases'. It is feasible to hold that every context or situation has its objective moral rules while also holding that what constitutes those rules is *relative* to the context or situation.

To claim that right and wrong are relative to a context is not to claim that anything goes. For objectivists who are also relativists, a clear understanding of a particular context dictates what is moral in that context. They hold, for example, that the rights and wrongs of killing in the context of war are *different* from the rights and wrongs of killing in the context of peace, but that the different moral rules functioning in each context are nonetheless very real.

As to the moral rules of war, international humanitarian law, based on theories of basic human rights, draws a distinction between *legitimate acts of war*, such as an armed combatant killing another armed combatant in battle, and *war crimes*, such as killing unarmed prisoners of war who have clearly surrendered. Of those who reject the distinction, a *warmonger* might argue that there are no rules of war, that war is war and anything goes. At the other extreme, a *pacifist* might argue that war is simply mutual mass murder because killing another human being can never be justified.

As we have seen, utilitarianism rejects moral absolutism, the idea that certain actions are intrinsically right or wrong, in favour of the idea that the same action can be right in some circumstances and wrong in others. Utilitarianism is nonetheless objective, if moral objectivism is at all possible, in so far as it maintains that the morality of particular actions can be objectively assessed according to the extent to which their consequences produce the greatest happiness.

In rejecting the notion that moral objectivism implies moral absolutism, and defending the notion that moral objectivism can be consistent with moral relativism, the British philosopher Renford Bambrough says:

> Many of the forms of moral scepticism that are special cases of sceptical theories of potentially wider scope are based on confusions between the concepts of relativity and subjectivity and those of absoluteness and objectivity. To suggest that there is a *right* answer to a moral problem is at once to be accused of or credited with a belief in moral absolutes. But it is no more necessary to believe in moral absolutes in order to believe in moral objectivity than it is to believe in the existence of absolute space or absolute time in order to believe in the objectivity of temporal and spatial relations and of judgements about them.
>
> *Moral Scepticism and Moral Knowledge*, pp. 32–3

Moral Subjectivism

Moral subjectivism, more broadly *moral scepticism*, scepticism about the objectivity of morality, goes back at least as far as the ancient Greeks. The pre-Socratic philosopher Protagoras, most famous for arguing that 'Man is the measure of all things' (quoted in Plato, *Theaetetus*, 152a, p. 30), held that there are as many different measures of goodness and badness as there are people, thus endorsing an extreme form of subjective ethical relativism.

It was, however, David Hume who most famously raised doubts about the very possibility of moral objectivism. We saw earlier how Hume, as a major exponent of empiricism, argues that there are no *ideas* in the mind that are not ultimately derived from sensory *impressions*. He uses this central thesis to argue that we do not actually possess certain ideas that we believe we possess because we receive no impressions to give rise to those ideas.

He argues, for example, that we have no idea of a *necessary causal connection* between events. We simply observe one event repeatedly following another, what he calls *constant conjunction*, and begin to suppose that the effect is somehow a necessary result of the cause. Our supposed idea of necessary connection is actually only an idea of constant junction because constant conjunction is all we ever have impressions of. By this line of reasoning Hume establishes a principle that has become a cornerstone of modern scientific method: that it is never necessary or inevitable that one event will produce another. We confidently expect heat to melt ice because we have always observed that connection in the past, but it is not logically necessary that heat will continue to melt ice in the future.

Similarly, Hume argues that we receive no impression of the goodness or badness, rightness or wrongness of a person, action or event. There are no *moral properties* to be observed alongside the *natural properties* that we observe. When I witness a stabbing, for example, I perceive the knife going in, the blood flowing and the cries of the victim, but I do not perceive the badness of the act. The supposition that goodness and badness are natural properties of persons, actions and events has come to be known as *naturalistic fallacy*, a term introduced by G. E. Moore in his 1903 book *Principia Ethica*.

In his *A Treatise of Human Nature*, Hume famously illustrates what later came to be known as naturalistic fallacy by comparing the crime of parricide with a sapling growing up to kill its parent tree by overtopping it and depriving it of light. He asks what the basis is for our conclusion that parricide is heinously immoral while overtopping is amoral and natural, if what we perceive in both cases is essentially the same: an offspring killing its parent. It is worth quoting Hume at length, not least because he is always a joy to read:

> Reason or science is nothing but the comparing of ideas, and the discovery of their relations; and if the same relations have different characters, it must evidently follow, that those characters are not

discover'd merely by reason. To put the affair, therefore, to this trial, let us chuse any inanimate object, such as an oak or elm; and let us suppose, that by the dropping of its seed, it produces a sapling below it, which springing up by degrees, at last overtops and destroys the parent tree: I ask, if in this instance there be wanting any relation, which is discoverable in parricide or ingratitude? Is not the one tree the cause of the other's existence; and the latter the cause of the destruction of the former, in the same manner as when a child murders his parent? 'Tis not sufficient to reply, that a choice or will is wanting. For in the case of parricide, a will does not give rise to any *different* relations, but is only the cause from which the action is deriv'd; and consequently produces the *same* relations, that in the oak or elm arise from some other principles. 'Tis a will or choice, that determines a man to kill his parent; and they are the laws of matter and motion, that determine a sapling to destroy the oak, from which it sprung. Here then the same relations have different causes; but still the relations are the same: And as their discovery is not in both cases attended with a notion of immorality, it follows, that that notion does not arise from such a discovery.

A Treatise of Human Nature, pp. 466–7

Hume also takes the example of our very different moral attitudes towards incest among humans and incest among animals. In the epic and sublime morality tale *Duncton Wood* (1980), by William Horwood, we are scandalized when the great mole Mandrake has intercourse with his daughter Rebecca, because the moles are so anthropomorphically portrayed. If there is, however, no difference between human and animal incest in terms of what they are in themselves and in terms of what we perceive, then on what basis do we proclaim the former to be morally repugnant and the later simply to be a part of nature?

Hume's all-important answer is that observing and reflecting upon cases of parricide and incest among humans stirs our *internal senses* and *sentiments* to feelings of *revulsion* and *disapproval*. On the other hand, observing and reflecting upon cases of, say, kindness and honesty among humans stirs our internal senses and sentiments to feelings of *delight* and *approval*.

In opposition to moral objectivism, Hume holds that we do not make moral distinctions on the basis of reason and cognition but upon the basis of *emotion*, *feeling* and *sentiment*. For Hume, morality is not rooted in the *cognitive* part of our nature but in the *conative*. That is, morality is not a matter of reason but a matter of desire and volition. It is because morality is a matter of desire and volition that it is capable of moving us to action. If it were merely a matter of cognition, of coldly understanding certain facts and having certain ideas, it would not be sufficient to motivate us to act.

Hume's answer to that key meta-ethical question 'Are there moral facts?' is a resounding 'No':

> Take any action allow'd to be vicious: Wilful murder, for instance. Examine it in all lights, and see if you can find that matter of fact, or real existence, which you call *vice*. In which-ever way you take it, you find only certain passions, motives, volitions and thoughts. There is no other matter of fact in the case. The vice entirely escapes you, as long as you consider the object. You never can find it, till you turn your reflection into your own breast, and find a sentiment of disapprobation, which arises in you, towards this action. Here is a matter of fact; but 'tis the object of feeling, not of reason. It lies in yourself, not in the object. So that when you pronounce any action or character to be vicious, you mean nothing, but that from the constitution of your nature you have a feeling or sentiment of blame from the contemplation of it.
>
> *A Treatise of Human Nature*, pp. 468–9

Hume goes on to note that authors of systems of morality are in the habit of making an illegitimate move from talking about what *is* and *is not* the case to talking about what *ought* and *ought not* to be the case, as though the mere *contemplation* of logical principles, metaphysical notions or the observable facts of an action or event were sufficient to furnish these authors with moral grounds for pronouncing that this principle *ought* to be applied or that this action *ought* to be performed or that this event *ought not* to take place.

> In every system of morality, which I have hitherto met with, I have always remark'd, that the author proceeds for some time in the ordinary way of reasoning, and establishes the being of a God, or makes observations concerning human affairs; when of a sudden I am surpriz'd to find, that instead of the usual copulations of propositions, *is*, and *is not*, I meet with no proposition that is not connected with an *ought*, or an *ought not*. This change is imperceptible; but is, however, of the last consequence. For as this *ought*, or *ought not*, expresses some new relation or affirmation, 'tis necessary that it shou'd be observ'd and explain'd; and at the same time that a reason should be given, for what seems altogether inconceivable, how this new relation can be a deduction from others, which are entirely different from it.
>
> *A Treatise of Human Nature*, p. 469

Hume holds that there is no legitimate way to move from an *is* statement or proposition to an *ought* statement or proposition. In short, that it is impossible to get an *ought* from an *is*. This has come to be known as *Hume's law*, the *is–ought problem* or the *is–ought gap*. The problem is rooted in the fact that, for Hume, *is* propositions are meaningful because they can be true or false, whereas *ought* propositions, moral propositions, are not meaningful because they cannot be true or false.

Hume holds that only two types of proposition are meaningful, *relations of ideas* and *matters of fact*. Hume's distinction between *relations of ideas* and *matters of fact* is today knows as *Hume's fork*.

Relations of ideas refers to all the purely logical relationships that are found, for example, in maths and geometry. The mind has the capacity to recognize that the idea '2 + 2', for example, is equivalent to the idea '4'. On this basis the mind can immediately conclude that the statement or proposition '2 + 2 = 4' is absolutely certain. The proposition 'A mother is a female parent' also expresses a relationship of ideas. Once a person has learnt what the terms 'mother' and 'female parent' mean, the truth of the proposition 'A mother is a female parent' is unavoidable.

Hume's *relations of ideas* are today called *analytic propositions*. Such propositions simply exhibit logic rather than any kind of metaphysical knowledge. As Hume says in his *An Enquiry Concerning Human Understanding* (1748), 'Propositions of this kind are discoverable by the mere operation of thought, without dependence on what is anywhere existent in the universe' (*An Enquiry Concerning Human Understanding*, p. 25).

Matters of fact include all those propositions that are held to be true on the basis of the present evidence of our senses or the evidence of past experience as recorded by our memory. 'The banana is yellow', 'The sea is blue', 'Paris is the capital of France' and so on. Hume's *matters of fact* are today called *synthetic propositions*. Most of our talking and thinking is made up of synthetic propositions.

It is because moral propositions are neither relations of ideas or matters of fact that they are, according to Hume, unable to be true or false and are essentially meaningless. They do not fit onto either prong of Hume's fork.

Let us return to the contemplation of Donald Trump's hair. The proposition 'Trump is blond', for example, expresses a matter of fact about Trump firmly established on the basis of empirical evidence. He may not be a natural blond, and it is hard to figure out exactly what is going on with that enigmatic hair, but nonetheless there is no getting away from the fact that the forty-fifth POTUS is blond.

The moral proposition 'Trump is wicked', however, does not express a matter of fact or falsehood about Trump because wickedness, according to Hume and others, is not part of the fabric of the world. As Nietzsche says in one of his pithy aphorisms, 'There are no moral phenomena at all, only a moral interpretation of phenomena' (*Beyond Good and Evil*, 108, p. 96). For Hume, that 'moral interpretation' is emotional not cognitive.

Neither does the proposition 'Trump is wicked' express a relation of ideas, because whatever Hillary Clinton's sour grapes lead her to believe, Trump is not synonymous with wickedness as 2 + 2 is synonymous with 4. At best, the grammatical construction, the pseudo-proposition with no truth value 'Trump is wicked' expresses *feelings* of disapprobation towards Trump, just as swearing or groaning at the sight of him does.

All these clever Humean ideas, naturalistic fallacy, is–ought gap, Hume's fork, were hugely influential on later moral subjectivists, and even on some moral objectivists who recognized that if they were to somehow construct a *tenable* objective moral theory they had to take on board the crux of what Hume is saying. *Hume's fork*, in particular, had a massive influence on a group of later philosophers called the *logical positivists* who, like Hume, were moral subjectivists.

Logical positivism was the brainchild of a group of philosophers who met regularly in Vienna in the years between the two world wars. The logical positivists of this now famous Vienna Circle were devout disciples of Hume. They undertook to develop Hume's ideas with the intention of cleaning up philosophy and rendering it compatible with the methods and principles of modern science.

A precocious young English philosopher, Sir Alfred Jules 'Freddie' Ayer, better known as A. J. Ayer, introduced himself to the Vienna Circle while on a postgraduate stay in Vienna in 1932. Recognizing his brilliance they soon welcomed him in. Already like-minded, it took little to convert Ayer to logical positivism, and just a few years later, at the age of only twenty-five, he wrote *Language, Truth and Logic* (1936), the book that introduced logical positivism to the English-speaking world.

It is the two sharp prongs of Hume's fork that most captivate the logical positivists. What are sometimes referred to as the two horns of Hume's *charging bull*. Hume being the quintessential bull in the china shop of old, dusty philosophical convention and old, crusty received opinion. At the heart of logical positivism is the *verification principle*.

What the verification principle is has already been more or less explained via the above explanation of Hume's fork. The short version of the principle is: 'All proposition are true, false or meaningless.' A longer formulation of the principle is: 'Propositions that cannot be verified as tautologies (A is A) or contradictions (A is not A) on the basis of pure logic, or verified as true or false on the basis of empirical evidence, are unverifiable and therefore meaningless.'

Logical positivists recognize that there are many synthetic propositions the truth or falsehood of which – the *truth value* of which – has not yet been established. For example, 'There was life on Mars.' They allow that such propositions are meaningful if they are *verifiable in principle*. That is, if it is empirically possible to establish their truth value even if nobody has yet done so.

Wielding the verification principle the logical positivists aimed to tidy up philosophy, indeed to tidy up all human reasoning. Logic and mathematics would remain on the one side, prong or horn, and empirical science would remain on the other. All other thinking that was neither purely logical nor purely scientific, such as metaphysics, ethics and aesthetics, would be cast aside as nonsense.

The most that these ancient areas of discourse could hope for in future was to be placed on a par with poetry; to be treated as collections of utterances, imperatives and exclamations expressing feelings, emotions, hopes and aspirations, rather than as collections of meaningful propositions stating facts and falsehoods.

In *Language, Truth and Logic*, Ayer echoes Hume as he emphatically proclaims the logical positivist position regarding ethics without pulling any punches:

> If now I generalise my previous statement and say, 'Stealing money is wrong,' I produce a sentence which has no factual meaning – that is, express no proposition which can be either true or false. It is as if I had written 'stealing money!!' – where the shape and thickness of the exclamation marks show, by a suitable convention, that a special sort of moral disapproval is the feeling which is being expressed. It is clear that there is nothing said here which can be true or false.
>
> *Language, Truth and Logic*, p. 110

Ayer is not in the business of advocating a pilfering free-for-all at the local department store, but instead making a serious positivist point about the epistemological status of moral propositions, such as 'Stealing money is wrong'. As this proposition is neither analytic or synthetic it must be meaningless, as must all moral propositions, all moral discourse. In the view of Ayer and others, moral propositions do not and cannot express facts. There are no moral facts. In fact, there are no genuine moral propositions. As he goes on to say:

> Another man may disagree with me about the wrongness of stealing, in the sense that he may not have the same feelings about stealing as I have, and he may quarrel with me on account of my moral sentiments. But he cannot, strictly speaking, contradict me. For in saying that a certain type of action is right or wrong, I am not making any factual statement, not even a statement about my own state of mind. I am merely expressing certain moral sentiments. And the man who is ostensibly contradicting me is merely expressing his moral sentiments. So that there is plainly no sense in asking which of us is in the right. For neither of us is asserting a genuine proposition.
>
> *Language, Truth and Logic*, pp. 110–11

Ayer is endorsing here a form of moral subjectivism or non-cognitivism know as *emotivism,* a position first put forward by Axel Hägerström, founder of the Uppsala School of Philosophy, the less well-known Swedish counterpart of the Vienna Circle.

Emotivists argue that although the disagreement between people on either side of the abortion issue, for example, is very real in terms of the animosity each side feels for the views and actions of the other, there is no solving the disagreement by moral argument because there are no moral facts of the matter to be discovered or worked out that could ever lead to the conclusion that one side is morally wrong and the other side morally right.

Those who are anti-abortion have strong *feelings* one way, those who are pro-abortion have strong *feelings* another way. According to emotivists, saying 'Abortion is wrong' is just a fancy way of exclaiming 'Abortion – boo!', while saying 'Abortion is acceptable' is just a fancy way of exclaiming 'Abortion – hooray!' Not surprisingly, emotivism has been given the silly but rather appropriate nickname of the 'boo–hooray' theory of ethics.

Some narrow-minded, reactionary types have claimed that it is immoral to claim, as Ayer does, that morality has no basis in fact, because to do so licenses people to do as they please. Claiming that morality has no basis in fact may well encourage some people to do as they please, but it is nonetheless very poor philosophizing indeed to insist that philosophers who think that morality has no basis in fact have a moral obligation to say that it does have a basis in fact. As Hume says:

> There is no method of reasoning more common, and yet none more blameable, than, in philosophical disputes, to endeavour the refutation of any hypothesis, by a pretence of its dangerous consequences to religion and morality. When any opinion leads to absurdities, it is certainly false, but it is not certain that an opinion is false because it is of dangerous consequence. Such topics, therefore, ought entirely to be forborne; as serving nothing to the discovery of truth, but only to make the person of an antagonist odious.
>
> *An Enquiry Concerning Human Understanding*, p. 96

Another form of moral subjectivism or non-cognitivism known as *prescriptivism* was put forward by the English moral philosopher R. M. Hare in his book *The Language of Morals* (1952). Hare notes that moral propositions often have a *descriptive*, denotive form. 'Stealing is wrong', for example, describes stealing as having the property of wrongness. Hare, however, agrees with Hume that moral properties such as wrongness and rightness, badness and goodness do not exist, and certainly that they are not perceivable features of the world.

When I witness a theft I perceive various natural properties. A person moving stealthily, looking about furtively, a hand emerging from an oversized sleeve to grasp an unguarded smartphone from a café table, the hand and the phone disappearing into the large sleeve and the person scurrying off with their ill-gotten gains, but I do not perceive the wrongness. If I supposed that I perceived the wrongness I would be committing the naturalistic fallacy.

For Hare, the *descriptive* form of moral propositions, a form that so often entices us into the snare of the naturalistic fallacy, masks the real *prescriptive* form of moral propositions. When a person says 'Stealing is wrong', apparently denoting a property of stealing, what they are really saying is 'Don't steal'. They are *prescribing* a course of action; issuing an action guiding imperative rather than stating a fact. They want others to act as they do and also perhaps to be consistent in their behaviour. 'You don't steal from your friends, so don't steal from that stranger.'

Prescriptivism is similar to emotivism in that both positions hold that when a person says 'Stealing is wrong', what is taking place is not a statement of fact but an expression of how the person speaking *feels* about stealing, that they disapprove of it, find it abhorrent and so on. Prescriptivism simply places more focus on what emotivism would also acknowledge, that a person voices their disapproval because they want the person or persons they are addressing to feel and act as they do.

Emotivists certainly recognize that when a person expresses positive or negative feelings about Trump, stealing or abortion they are seeking to engender the same feelings in others. For emotivists, moral terms like wrong, bad, wicked, right, good and virtuous are *emotive* terms uttered with the aim of arousing feelings. As every great political orator and skilled politician knows, it is impossible to get anyone to do anything unless you first rouse their positive and negative feelings and engage their enthusiasm.

Nihilism is belief in nothing to the point of despair, and extreme scepticism about the possibility of moral knowledge can certainly lead to *moral nihilism*. A consistent moral subjectivist might well disapprove of concentration camps as against those who approve of them and so on, but he would recognize that there is no hope of solving moral issues through the promotion of reason and common sense and the removal of ignorance and prejudice, although he might vaguely hope that issues cease to be issues by everyone in the world coming to share his disapproval of certain practices and his approval of others.

For a consistent moral subjectivist, there would be no fox-hunting issue if everyone disapproved of fox hunting, there would be no paedophilia issue if everyone approved of paedophilia. Paedophilia is so widely and intensely disapproved of that the very suggestion that it would no longer be a moral issue if everyone approved of it is itself shocking. That shock highlights the difficulty of being a consistent moral nihilist.

Being a consistent moral nihilist is rather like being a consistent causal determinist or solipsist. It is all well and good claiming to be a determinist, solipsist or moral nihilist, but professed belief in these extreme sceptical positions always breaks down in practice.

Unfortunately, in saying this I seem to be in danger of falling into insisting that there must be such things as objective moral standards because we cannot do without them and will always in the end demand them, a position that I declared a few paragraphs ago, along with Hume, to be very poor philosophizing indeed.

All a philosopher concerned about the nihilistic implications of moral subjectivism can reasonably do is to keep searching for and making a sensible case for genuine forms of moral objectivism that also address or accommodate Hume's key points. This is the approach of the moral philosopher and consistent critic of moral subjectivism Mary Warnock, who once said:

> Without *some* element of objectivity, without *any* criterion for preferring one scheme of values to another, except the criterion of what looks most attractive to oneself, there cannot in fact be any morality at all, and moral theory must consist only in the assertion that there is no morality.
>
> *Existentialist Ethics*, p. 56

Not prepared to be an ivory tower philosopher, Warnock's career showed an intense interest in public affairs. She always sought to use her common-sense moral and philosophical wisdom to positively sway public and social policy, particularly in the areas of education, medical ethics and animal rights.

Her involvement in real-world ethical issues, where moral theories and decisions literally make the difference between life and death for real people, led her to be critical of those bookish, pedantic, university philosophers who treat ethics as though it were nothing more than a game of chess, while trivializing real-world moral concerns with their analytic, linguistic, positivistic, ivory tower approach.

I am somewhat guilty of such trivializing myself no doubt, with my deliberately amusing or outrageous examples and so forth. But for all that, I have not forgotten that ethics is a serious business. Neither should you.

Back to Moral Objectivism: Just a Little Moore

One philosopher who seeks to make a case for moral objectivism, in the full glare of Hume's sceptical roasting of the very notion, is G. E. Moore. Moore understood Hume's position on ethics so well that it was he and not Hume who coined the phrase *naturalistic fallacy* to describe one of the central errors that Hume exposes in his attack upon moral objectivism. My reason for outlining Moore's objectivist position now rather than earlier is that his position is best understood in light of Hume's position, in light of an understanding of naturalistic fallacy.

George Edward Moore has an exceptional philosophical pedigree. Professor of Philosophy at the University of Cambridge he was a colleague of Bertrand Russell and Ludwig Wittgenstein, both of whom he influenced to a considerable degree. His ideas remain influential across several areas of philosophy, not least ethics. *Principia Ethica*, probably his best-known work, was a major inspiration to the Bloomsbury Set of Virginia Woolf et al., who adored the close comparison the book draws between ethics and aesthetics.

The Latin term *principia* means *principles, especially first or fundamental principles*. To use the term is to evoke Isaac Newton's world-shattering *Philosophiæ Naturalis Principia Mathematica* of 1687. The term is somehow unavoidably pretentious, so if you are going to use it in the title of your book you had better know exactly what you are talking about. Alfred North Whitehead and Bertrand Russell, who knew exactly what they were talking about, used the term in the title of their seminal work *Principia Mathematica* (1910–13).

Written around the same time as *Principia Mathematica*, in the same location and intellectual environment, although published seven years earlier, *Principia Ethica* undertakes to do for ethics what Whitehead and Russell were undertaking to do for logic and maths; that is, establish and clarify first principles and remove long-standing confusions.

Much of Moore's *Principia* is taken up with exploring, in exhaustive detail, Hume's insight that most systems of morality are guilty of naturalistic fallacy. Moore expands on Hume's insight not least by levelling the charge of naturalistic fallacy against systems of morality that succeeded Hume, particularly the hedonistic utilitarianism of Bentham and Mill, even though that moral theory is, in ways already explored, very much a product of the empiricism of Hume.

Moore argues that the fundamental naturalistic error of hedonistic utilitarianism is to equate *goodness* with *pleasure*. If goodness and pleasure are taken to be the same thing then to assert that 'Pleasure is good' is to say no more than 'Good is good', which is really to say nothing. The equation does not define *good* and certainly we are no nearer to understanding what good is.

Someone might object that we all know what pleasure is and pleasure is precisely what is good as opposed to bad. Simples. Moore tackles this kind of seemingly common-sense response with what is known as the *open-question argument*, in which he maintains that questions about what is good and what good is are never *closed questions* but always *open questions*, always questions the answer to which is *open to debate*. Let us back up a little in order to get sufficient momentum to run through a full explanation of this one.

Moore's colleague Russell identifies what he calls *barren tautologies*. For example, 'A quadruped is a four footed animal.' This proposition is true by definition. 'Quadruped' simply means 'four-footed animal.' The proposition is barren because if you know what 'quadruped' means you already know it means 'four-footed animal'. No new information is conveyed.

Although not all closed questions arise from barren tautologies, barren tautologies always give rise to *closed* questions. Any type of closed question can be fully answered either with a straightforward 'yes' or 'no' or by providing a specific piece of information. Take the closed question, 'Where is the sugar?' The sugar is where it is, so the answer 'It is in the cupboard' will be either true or false. The tautology-inspired closed question 'Is a quadruped a four-footed animal?' also has a definite answer. In this case, if you understand what a quadruped is, and your intention is to respond sensibly, you have absolutely no choice but to answer 'Yes'.

An *open* question, on the other hand, is one that cannot be answered either with a straightforward 'yes' or 'no' or by providing a specific piece of information. There is scope for debate. An open question certainly cannot be answered simply on the basis of an understanding of the terms within the question.

For example, 'Are dogs clever?' is an open question. The terms 'dog' and 'clever' are not synonymous, dogs are not *by definition* clever, and a definite answer to this question cannot be given simply on the basis of an understanding of the terms within it. Indeed, a definite answer cannot be given to this question at all. Dog lovers will argue that dogs are clever, citing wonderful examples of doggy intelligence, while others will argue that a dog has never won the Nobel Prize for Physics.

Now, according to Moore 'Is pleasure good?' is also an open question. The terms 'pleasure' and 'good' are not synonymous, pleasure is not *by definition* good. People who understand the terms within the question can and do disagree about the answer to it, revealing that good cannot be defined as pleasure as a quadruped can be defined as a four-footed animal.

Exactly the same can be said for the question 'Is happiness good?', or for any question whatsoever with the form 'Is x good?' Any question concerning the nature or definition of goodness is always an open question, revealing that no x is synonymous with good. Or to put it another way, good is not synonymous with any *predicate* x.

A *predicate* is that part of a proposition which identifies a property belonging to the *subject* of the proposition. In the proposition 'Grass is green', for example, 'grass' is the subject term while 'green' is the predicate term. As good is not synonymous with any predicate x, as there is no predicate that can stand for good, good cannot be a property of anything. In short, goodness does not exist, at least as a natural property of anything.

Moore concludes that goodness cannot be defined, that it is indefinable. He does not, however, conclude that goodness does not exist. For Moore, although goodness does not exist as a *natural property*, it nonetheless exists as a *non-natural property*; a metaphysical, transcendent quality that is not available to the senses but is rather intuited by the intellect, or even, according to some readings of Moore, by a specific *moral faculty*. This is known as Moore's *intuitionism*. The non-natural moral property of goodness is comparable to, and for Moore closely akin to, the non-natural *aesthetic* property of *beauty*.

What was said about goodness in our consideration of the open-question argument can also be said about beauty. Beauty is not synonymous with anything with which it is commonly identified: symmetry, purity, elegance, loveliness and so on. You might think that when, for example, you perceive a statue widely held to be beautiful, you perceive its beauty alongside its natural properties of symmetry, proportion, elegance, whiteness, coldness, hardness and smoothness. But really its beauty is a property of a different order, a property that *transcends* the physical properties, a property that can be alluded to, as I am alluding to it now, but cannot be directly pointed out or defined.

The beauty of a beautiful statue, painting, woman, man, house, bridge or mountain requires a combination of natural properties, because without the natural properties the beautiful thing would not exist. However, the beauty of a thing is not one of its natural properties but rather a non-natural property that *transcends* the natural properties. In the same way, the non-natural property of goodness *transcends* the natural objects, emotions, actions, attitudes and habits that we hold to be most valuable and broadly describe as good.

It is perhaps ironic that Moore, after developing to the full Hume's insight vis-à-vis naturalistic fallacy, ends up endorsing what can be seen as an exotic metaphysics of non-natural properties existing in a supersensible dimension intuited by some higher intellectual faculty. Hume, who condemns all metaphysical writings as containing 'nothing but sophistry and illusion' (*An Enquiry Concerning Human Understanding*, p. 165), would not approve at all, although Plato almost certainly would.

Towards the end of *Principia Ethica* Moore advocates *ideal utilitarianism*, a variant of consequentialism already considered in the previous chapter. *Intrinsic value*, he says, does not belong to pleasure or even to happiness, but to *consciousness* of beauty and friendship.

Of all things in life consciousness of beauty and consciousness of friendship are the most valuable, 'worth having purely *for their own sakes*' (*Principia Ethica*, 113, p. 188) and not merely for the sake of something else. These things are not synonymous with goodness but they are the highest goods. Highest in the sense of being the most valuable things in human life and, therefore, the things that should be pursued and promoted above all else, the ends to which all else should be a means. I give Moore the final word, at length:

> By far the most valuable things, which we know or can imagine, are certain states of consciousness, which may be roughly described as the pleasures of human intercourse and the enjoyment of beautiful objects. No one, probably, who has asked himself the question, has ever doubted that personal affection and appreciation of what is beautiful in Art or Nature, are good in themselves; nor, if we consider strictly what things are worth having *purely for their own sakes*, does it appear probable that any one will think that anything else has *nearly* so great a value as the things

which are included under these two heads. I have myself urged that the mere existence of what is beautiful does appear to have *some* intrinsic value; but I regard it as indubitable that . . . such mere existence of what is beautiful has value, so small as to be negligible, in comparison with that which attaches to the *consciousness* of beauty. This simple truth may, indeed, be said to be universally recognised. What has *not* been recognised is that it is the ultimate and fundamental truth of Moral Philosophy. That it is only for the sake of these things—in order that as much of them as possible may at some time exist—that anyone can be justified in performing any public or private duty.

Principia Ethica, 113, pp. 188–9

4
GOODNESS AT ISSUE

This chapter is about *applied ethics*. Applied ethics, also called *practical ethics*, is concerned with the practical application of normative moral theories to actual, real world moral issues, with the aim of clarifying or even solving those moral issues. There are many moral issues, many ongoing and often heated ethical debates, in the areas of medicine, ecology, war, recreational drugs, famine relief, punishment, gender equality, pornography, censorship and so on.

Many so-called moral issues actually boil down to disputes about *facts*. The angry debate surrounding the existence of nuclear weapons, for example, is really an argument about facts. There is little or no debate as to whether or not it is a bad thing to incinerate millions of people with nuclear weapons. The debate centres instead around what is most likely to ensure that nuclear weapons are never used in combat again: the possession of nuclear weapons by superpowers, giving rise to the deterrent of mutually assured destruction (MAD), or the worldwide abolition of nuclear weapons?

Obviously, if the world could get rid of all its nuclear weapons they could not be used, but is it at all realistic to believe that this could ever be achieved in a world where every nation is at least wary of the possibility that it could be attacked by its neighbours? Moreover, although it is said that people who live in glasshouses should not throw stones, a nation with a lack of confidence in its defences is often more likely to be motivated by Hobbesian *diffidence* (*Leviathan*, pp. 184–5) to make pre-emptive or preventive strikes than a well-defended nation. Is any nation, therefore, ever likely to settle for bows and arrows when its neighbour has, or could reacquire, cannon? To abolish nuclear weapons is difficult, to un-invent them impossible.

In undermining the principle of MAD, would *unilateral* nuclear disarmament, as a hopeful step towards comprehensive *multilateral* nuclear disarmament, actually make the world less safe? Would all-out, direct, conventional warfare between superpowers be more likely in a world without nuclear weapons? As said, the dispute is over *facts* between two sides neither of which want nuclear war.

My aim, actually, is not to be drawn into commenting on a host of moral issues. There are so many of them that at least another book would be required just to explore the main ones. Rather, I shall examine just two contentious moral issues in the area of taking and preserving life, two issues that are in some ways, as you will see, quite closely related: *abortion* and *animal rights*.

These two important moral issues are hard fought on both sides and as a result receive a great deal of emotive media coverage. They are familiar to us all, even if most people, including many of those directly involved in campaigning for one side or the other, are less familiar with the finer philosophical details of the various arguments than they could be.

In choosing these two issues my aim is not only to shed light on them for the sake of it, but perhaps primarily to introduce several key moral concepts that help to clarify matters across a wide range of debates within applied ethics. What these key moral concepts are will emerge as we go forward, but they are certainly ideas and distinctions that you can usefully add to your own burgeoning ethical toolkit.

The Abortion Issue

Biological and Legal Background

The *moral* debate concerning abortion is better understood in light of the following basic *biological* and *legal* information concerning abortion.

When a human male sperm cell fuses with a human female egg cell or ovum the fertilized ovum begins to cleave repeatedly to form a collection of cells called a *zygote*. Five days on from conception the zygote, having acquired two different cell components and a fluid cavity, becomes a *blastocyst* which on about day six implants itself into the uterine wall.

Twelve days on from conception, placental blood circulation begins and the blastocyst is said to have become an *embryo*. The embryonic stage is marked by *differentiation*: the formation of the various cell types that comprise the different components of the organism. By week five the now peanut-shaped embryo has a detectable heartbeat and has begun to acquire a distinctive morphology, a head and tiny buds that will grow into arms and legs.

By the end of week ten, although the embryo is still less than two inches long from crown to rump, it has acquired a distinctively human morphology and most of its bodily systems are in place, at least at a basic level. From the start of week eleven until birth the organism is described as a *foetus*. The average length of human gestation is 280 days or forty weeks or roughly nine months. Not until the foetus is born should it be formally described as a *baby*, even though a baby born prematurely is less developed than a foetus that has reached full term.

As a result of ever advancing medical technology there are a few instances of premature babies of between 21 and 22 weeks gestation surviving, the youngest possibly being 21 weeks and 4 days gestation, although such figures are dependent upon when the precise start of the gestation period is taken to be.

A premature baby is said to be *viable* if it has at least a 50 per cent chance of survival outside the womb. Clearly, the *viabilit*y of a premature baby depends to a large extent on how advanced the medical technology is in the place where it is born, but the current limit anywhere is about twenty-four weeks. A baby of twenty-four weeks' gestation that survives runs a high risk of neonatal morbidity and ongoing health issues. Generally, medical practitioners will not provide intensive care for a baby of twenty-three weeks' gestation but will for a baby of twenty-six weeks' gestation.

An *abortion* is an induced termination of a pregnancy resulting in the destruction of the embryo or foetus. Modern, safe, professional methods involve medication or surgery. Traditional methods involve herbal medicines, sharp tools or severely traumatizing the embryo or foetus in some less direct way. In 2017, the World Health Organization, an agency of the United Nations, estimated that 45 per cent of the abortions taking place in the world annually are still carried out unsafely.

The estimated number of abortions taking place in the world increased from 50 million a year in the early 1990s to 56 million a year during the period 2010 to 2014. This *overall* worldwide increase is entirely due to population growth, with abortion *rates* as a percentage of pregnancies *decreasing* in most places, particularly in the developed world, largely due to better and more widely available contraception reducing the percentage of unwanted pregnancies. Approximately 88 per cent of all abortions now take place in the developing world.

As to abortion law, it varies widely around the world in the degree to which it permits or prohibits abortion. A few strongly Catholic countries, mostly in Latin America and the Caribbean, but also Malta and Vatican City, prohibit abortion without exception, although the law tends not to be strictly enforced where pregnancy threatens the woman's life. In many countries abortion is *legal on request* within a certain number of weeks of gestation. In many other countries abortion is legal within a certain number of weeks of gestation but is subject to a range of restrictions.

In the United Kingdom, for example, abortion is restricted to cases of maternal life, health, mental health, rape, foetal defects and/or socioeconomic factors. As a reasonable case can always be made that at least one of these conditions is met, an abortion is effectively available in the UK, within a certain number of weeks, to any woman who needs or wants one. At the opposite end of the allowed but restricted scale, some countries, many of them in Africa, allow abortion only where maternal life is threatened.

In those countries that allow abortion to a lesser or greater extent, the number of weeks within which abortion is allowed varies widely from one country to the next and even from one state to the next. In the United Kingdom, for example, subject to the restrictions considered above, abortion is legal within twenty-four weeks and illegal thereafter, except in cases of extreme foetal abnormality or severe risk to the physical or mental well-being of the mother.

In the USA, for example, where abortion is currently legal on request and most states are content to draw their lines at various points between twenty-two and twenty-six weeks, some states are seeking to significantly reduce the number of weeks at which the legal line is drawn or even to impose a near-total ban. In March 2019 Utah, for example, passed a law prohibiting abortion beyond eighteen weeks. This law is currently blocked by a federal court injunction issued in accordance with *Roe v. Wade*, a landmark ruling made by the U.S. Supreme Court in 1973 that upholds a woman's constitutional right to have an abortion prior to the viability of the foetus.

The current trend in significant parts of the USA is towards more restrictive abortion laws and practices, with *Roe v. Wade* itself at risk of being overturned. For example, in May 2019 Alabama passed the Human Life Protection Act, outlawing abortion in almost all cases with effect from November 2019, although the enactment of this law is almost certain to be prevented by legal challenges, at least for some time. The Human Life Protection Act is specifically designed to work its way up to the U.S. Supreme Court as a challenge to *Roe v. Wade*. The current legal situation in the USA regarding abortion is extremely complex and I have only been able to give you a flavour of it here.

Many countries and states within countries draw their legal line at or around twenty-four weeks, although a few countries have no time limit for legal abortion. In Canada, for example, abortion is not only legal on request but also legal at any point during pregnancy. All abortion was illegal in Canada prior to 1969, but today Canada has no legal restrictions on abortion.

Despite the legal position, however, Canadian physicians follow strict professional guidelines that prohibit them from terminating a pregnancy beyond twenty-four weeks unless there are clear indications that the mother is at risk or the foetus is seriously malformed. The vast majority of abortions in Canada are carried out at an early stage of pregnancy, not least because women who need or want an abortion will almost always seek to undergo the procedure sooner rather than later. It is a plain fact that abortions are simpler and safer the earlier they are carried out.

Seeking to counter the myth that Canada is a land of late-term abortions, Dr Carolyn Bennett told the *National Post* on 5 February 2013, in an article titled 'Late-term Abortions Are Not Happening in Canada Without a "Reason"', that it is false to assert that late-term abortions can be carried out in Canada for any or no reason.

The Anti-abortion, Pro-life or Conservative Position

In his influential book *Practical Ethics* (1979), the Australian philosopher Peter Singer points out that 'the dispute about abortion is often taken to be a dispute about when human life begins' (*Practical Ethics*, p. 107). Singer says the *anti-abortion*, *pro-life* or *conservative* position centres around the following argument:

First premise: It is wrong to kill an innocent human being.

Second premise: A foetus is an innocent human being.

Conclusion: Therefore it is wrong to kill a human foetus.

Although the zygote is a minute clump of cells with no nervous system with which to feel anything, which often fails to implant in the uterine wall, conservatives are correct when they argue that there is a smooth continuum of development from zygote to baby. They go on to argue that there is, therefore, no 'morally significant dividing line' (*Practical Ethics*, p. 107) at which point it can be said that the organism *becomes* a human being.

Now, if there is no morally significant dividing line then we either reduce the moral status of babies to that of zygotes or raise the moral status of zygotes to that of babies; the moral status of babies being that although the Spartans left weak ones on the hillside to die, infanticide is today all but universally condemned as murder. So, if deliberately killing a baby is murder, and there is a smooth continuum of development from zygote to baby with no morally significant dividing line, then, according to conservatives, deliberately killing a zygote, embryo or foetus is also murder.

Those who question the claim that there is no morally significant dividing line offer three possibilities: i) *quickening*, ii) *viability* and iii) *birth*.

i) *Quickening* is the moment when movement of the foetus is first felt by the mother. It was widely held, particularly within the Catholic tradition, that quickening was the moment when the foetus acquired a soul and became fully human rather than a mere soulless animal. The notion of quickening is now dismissed as superstition even by the Catholic Church. The foetus was alive before 'quickening' and moving undetected. Recall that even by week five a human embryo has a heartbeat, so, at the very least, its heart was already moving. Stripped of its supposed religious significance, quickening comes down to nothing more than detectable movement. Being unable to move, however, does not cancel out a claim to go on living, otherwise completely paralysed human beings could be terminated with impunity.

ii) *Viability*, as we have seen, is the moment when a foetus has at least a 50 per cent chance of surviving outside the womb. As we have also seen, viability depends to a large extent on the availability of medical technology. Modern hospitals with state of the art equipment and procedures now enable very premature babies to survive that would simply not have been viable several decades ago. Are we to say that an abortion at a certain number of weeks of gestation was morally acceptable fifty years ago because the foetus was not viable, but is not morally acceptable today because the foetus is viable?

Exactly the same can be said for viability that is dependent on the varying quality of medical facilities in different locations. Singer highlights the absurdity of viability as a morally significant dividing line by pointing out how ridiculous it would be for a woman to travel from New York City to a village in New Guinea in order to render a foetus that would be viable in New York *unviable*, so that she could then have an abortion that she felt was morally acceptable (*Practical Ethics*, p. 109).

Many people still struggle, however, with the fact that a lot of countries allow abortions to take place beyond the current limit of viability of about twenty-four weeks. That is, they struggle with the fact that some very premature babies are surviving while at the same time slightly more developed foetuses are being legally aborted. Despite viability not being a good morally significant dividing line it certainly influences decisions to set the legal limit at about twenty-four weeks. On its own website, the Government of the Netherlands, for example, says, 'An abortion may be performed up to the time when the foetus is viable outside the mother's body. Under the Criminal Code, this is 24 weeks' (Government of the Netherlands, 'Legal time limit for abortion', www.government.nl/topics/abortion/question-and-answer/what-is-the-time-limit-for-having-an-abortion, 2018).

The setting of the twenty-four-week legal limit is not only influenced by viability, however, but by scientific evidence regarding the capacity of the foetus to feel pain or have any awareness whatsoever of its own existence. The scientific evidence is currently inconclusive, allowing both sides of the abortion debate to select from the research what best supports their case.

Some evidence suggests that an embryo of eight weeks has pain receptors, but it does not follow that it has a brain sufficiently developed to be conscious of any signals that these pain receptors may be sending. Grass responds to sunlight and a thermostat to heat but no one seriously maintains that they are conscious or aware of what they are responding to. Interestingly, the state of Utah currently requires a foetus of twenty weeks' gestation to be anesthetized prior to abortion because it *may* be able to feel pain.

Other research suggests that a foetus has no capacity to feel pain, because no consciousness, until the *third trimester*, which starts at about twenty-seven weeks. That very premature babies of less than twenty-four weeks' gestation are surviving outside the womb as a result of highly advanced medical technology does not necessarily imply that they feel pain or indeed pleasure or have any awareness whatsoever of their own existence during the early neonatal period. This is a highly emotive subject, particularly for parents of very premature babies and for women requiring an abortion close to or beyond twenty-four weeks. Hopefully, more light than heat will be shed on this matter as our exploration of the abortion issue as a whole proceeds.

iii) *Birth*. For *pro-choice* liberals, who hold that a woman's right to choose what happens to her own body should always override all other considerations, birth is the only morally significant dividing line. Pro-choice advocates accept that a late-term foetus is a human being but that this is irrelevant. We will look further at their position shortly.

The conservative response is to argue that the foetus and the baby are the same entity, one just happens to be inside the womb, the other outside. Moreover, given that a baby born prematurely is less developed than a foetus that has reached full term, why should it be acceptable to kill the latter when it is wrong to kill the former? Being inside or outside the womb ought to have no bearing on the rightness or wrongness of killing a human being.

The Pro-abortion, Pro-choice or Liberal Position

Many pro-abortion liberals do not challenge the second premise of the conservative argument that the foetus is an innocent human being. They nonetheless hold that abortion is acceptable. They offer a variety of reasons and arguments.

Although the abortion rate is declining in many places and overall, abortions will continue to happen so long as there are unwanted or harmful pregnancies. Abortion is a fact of life and women will continue to have abortions regardless of the law. Abortion laws that are overly prohibitive simply drive the practice of abortion underground, into the proverbial back streets, which only adds to the difficulties and risks that women with unwanted pregnancies must face.

Abortion must therefore be legal, liberals argue, because 'A law that has more bad effects than good ones is a bad law' (*Report of the Royal Commission on the Status of Women in Canada*, Chapter 4: 'Women and the Family', 240, p. 286). Moreover, the best possible medical services must be available to carry out abortions in order to minimize the physical and psychological risks they pose to women.

Some say this is not strictly a *moral* argument, but rather a *practical* one. A person can, for example, consistently maintain that abortion is wrong, never have an abortion themselves for that reason and counsel others to do the same, while also maintaining that for practical reasons abortion should be legally available on request. Against those who want to draw this strong distinction between the moral and the practical, it can be argued that a social practice that is truly practical and sensible *is* moral, morality being, as we have seen several times in this book already, essentially a matter of the rules that enable societies to function.

Thinking along these lines a utilitarian might well argue that a society that allows and facilitates abortion promotes the greatest happiness, while a society that outlaws and impedes it creates unnecessary unhappiness and distress. This argument may, however, be somewhat disregarding the happiness, or at least the *future* happiness, of the aborted foetus.

Responding to the utilitarian, the conservative will counter that moral considerations should always override practical ones, and that there is no greater moral consideration than that concerning the sanctity of human life. Abortion is the deliberate killing of an innocent human being and therefore all measures should be taken to prevent it and reduce the demand for it. The conservative refuses to rest in face of the claim that prohibiting abortion is impractical and dangerous, insisting that the situation can and must change.

The conservative who upholds the sanctity of human life is still confronted by the dilemma of what to do when a woman will die if she does not have an abortion. The most hard-line conservatives argue that Nature or God should be left to take its course, while less hard-line conservatives allow that the right to life of the mother outweighs the right to life of the foetus. In having an abortion the mother can be considered to be acting in self-defence.

As we have seen, many countries with very restrictive abortion laws nonetheless permit abortion where the woman's life is at risk, although in reality it may be difficult or impossible for those with limited resources to obtain a safe abortion in these countries. As to those few invariably Catholic countries that piously prohibit abortion without exception, they tend, fortunately but hypocritically, not to strictly enforce the law in cases where the woman's life was at risk. It is noted that in the European Union tiny island nation of Malta, for example, where there is a monument to the unborn child, abortion is illegal *de jure* but not *de facto*.

Another well-known liberal argument maintains that abortion belongs to a realm of *private morality*. The law and those who hold abortion to be immoral, therefore, have no business dictating what a pregnant woman ought to do. To have or not to have an abortion is her own personal moral decision.

We saw in the previous chapter, however, that the notion of a private morality is difficult to make sense of given that its so-called rules are arbitrary. Arguably, to be worthy of the name, a moral code must have objective rules that are applicable to everyone in similar circumstances regardless of their personal inclinations.

Perhaps aware that the notion of a private morality is problematic, liberals change tack somewhat and evoke Mill's *harm principle*, which we considered earlier: 'The only purpose for which power can be rightfully exercised over any member of a civilised community, against his will, is to prevent harm to others' (*On Liberty*, p. 14). Liberals argue that however much many people may disapprove of abortion, society has no right to prevent a woman from having an abortion because the activity causes no harm to others. They wish to see abortion included in the list of those practices that when outlawed give rise to *victimless crimes*.

Homosexuality, for example, given that its practice causes no harm to others, is a victimless crime in those places where it is still illegal. It is also argued by liberals that recreational drug taking, where illegal, is a victimless crime because its practice causes no harm to others. The counter-argument is of course that the taking of certain drugs in certain circumstances does cause harm to others: a heroin addict parent neglecting his children for example.

Gambling, where illegal, is also often considered to be a victimless crime, although excessive gambling by those who cannot afford it clearly has a detrimental effect on any financial dependants they may have. An occasional flutter harms no one and national lotteries do a great deal of good, while gambling addiction is often socially damaging.

The big problem with seeking to include abortion in the list of victimless crimes, as you may have already figured out for yourself, is that much of the abortion dispute is precisely about whether or not abortion has a victim, namely the aborted foetus. Conservatives will simply not accept that abortion has no victim, while liberals will either have to show that the foetus, although certainly killed, is not a victim in any truly meaningful sense of the term, or find other arguments in support of abortion that do not hinge on Mill's harm principle.

In modern times the abortion issue has become intimately entangled with the broader issue of *women's rights* and the cause of *feminism* in general, so much so that today the *pro-abortion* lobby is often called, and often is, the *pro-choice* lobby. *Pro-choice* refers, as said, to a woman's right to choose what happens to her own body at any point during her pregnancy to the exclusion of all other considerations. The pro-choice, feminist position does not deny that the foetus is an innocent human being or even that, if aborted, it is a victim, but it nonetheless insists that all this is irrelevant.

A key founder and staunch advocate of this position is the American feminist philosopher Judith Jarvis Thomson, who, in 1971, published a cleverly argued, highly influential and controversial academic paper called 'A Defense of Abortion'. In that paper, Thomson defends her strong pro-choice position with the following elaborate analogy:

You wake up in the morning and find yourself back to back in bed with an unconscious violinist. A famous unconscious violinist. He has been found to have a fatal kidney ailment, and the Society of Music Lovers has canvassed all the available medical records and found that you alone have the right blood type to help. They have therefore kidnapped you, and last night the violinist's circulatory system was plugged into yours, so that your kidneys can be used to extract poisons from his blood as well as your own.

'A Defense of Abortion', pp. 48–9

The director of the hospital says he would never have allowed you to be used in this way had he known. However, now that the violinist is connected he will die if he is disconnected within nine months. After nine months he will be able to survive without using you as a life-support machine. There is certainly a strong parallel here with pregnancy due to rape, where a woman is not responsible for her situation.

Singer, however, argues that Thomson's analogy can be easily adapted to cover cases of pregnancy that are not due to rape (*Practical Ethics*, p. 115). Suppose out of ignorance or carelessness you accidentally wonder into a ward where people volunteer to be used as life-support machines for other people, and before you know it you are sedated and plugged in. Arguably, nine months spent as an unwilling life-support machine is a high price to pay for ignorance or carelessness. Indeed, however you came to be in that situation, to be expected to remain in it is arguably morally unacceptable if at any point you decide that you do not want to remain in it.

For her part, Thomson asks, 'Is it morally incumbent on you to accede to this situation? No doubt it would be very nice of you if you did, a great kindness. But do you *have* to accede to it? ('A Defense of Abortion', p. 49). Her short answer is, of course, 'No'. She argues that although the violinist, the foetus, is an innocent human being with a *right to life*, this right to life does not impose on you a *duty* to save that life by any means whatsoever, however inconvenient those means are to you personally.

Thomson reinforces her point by arguing that a film star is not *morally* obliged to travel halfway around the world to lay his hand on your fevered brow, even if that is the only way to dispel your fever and save your life. It would be very generous of him to make the journey but he does not have to and nobody can reasonable expect him to do so on moral grounds. Recall Joseph Butler's arguments, considered in Chapter 2, that there are reasonable limits to altruism.

So, the violinist's right to life does not outweigh your right to unplug yourself if you so choose. The violinist's right to life does not include the right to expect you to remain plugged in. Few people would disagree with this if the violinist and his supporters were demanding that he remain plugged in to you for decades, for the personal imposition would be far more stark. The duration, however, is not the issue, but rather that he has no right to impose on you in that way for any length of time and that you have every right not to be imposed on in that way. In short, his right to life, a foetus's right to life, does not entail a right to use your body.

> The right to life consists not in the right not to be killed, but rather in the right not to be killed unjustly. This runs a risk of circularity, but never mind: it would enable us to square the fact that the violinist has a right to life with the fact that you do not act unjustly towards him in unplugging yourself, thereby killing him. For if you do not kill him unjustly, you do not violate his right to life, and so it is no wonder you do him no injustice.

> 'A Defense of Abortion', p. 57

In allowing that actions can be justified *independently* of their consequences, in arguing that we are not always obliged to do whatever has the best consequences, indeed that in certain circumstances we have *the right not to do* whatever has the best consequences, Thomson's position is anti-utilitarian.

Against Thomson, an *act* utilitarian might well argue that because allowing the violinist to remain plugged in to you contributes to the greatest happiness, it is wrong to unplug the violinist. Remaining plugged in might well be inconvenient and annoying to you, but it is only for nine months and will certainly make the violinist, his family and his music-loving followers extremely happy.

With regard to pregnancy, it may not be as obvious as it is in the case of the violinist that remaining plugged in to the foetus contributes to the greatest happiness. The various *benefits* of an abortion to the mother and perhaps also to her dependants have to be weighed against any *disbenefits*, perhaps the suffering of the foetus or the loss of its future happiness or the unhappiness of those who desired its birth.

For his part, a *rule* utilitarian might well argue that it detracts from the greatest happiness to have a world in which people are expected to serve against their will as life-support machines for others. People should not be expected, therefore, to serve against their will as life-support machines for others, however pleasing the outcome might be to some people on particular occasions. Thus, a *rule* utilitarian might well arrive at roughly the same conclusion as Thomson, albeit via a very different route following very different principles.

Humans, Persons, Speciesism and Morally Relevant Characteristics

So far, none of the pro-abortion liberal arguments that we have considered have challenged the *first* premise of the conservative position: 'It is wrong to kill an innocent human being.' Thomson may appear to challenge this premise but note that she adheres to the principle that a human being has a right to life, a right not to be *unjustly* killed. In her view, a foetus is an innocent human being that would be unjustly killed if anyone but the mother, with her overriding right to choose what happens to her own body, chose to kill it.

It is hardly surprising that the first premise of the conservative position has so far gone unchallenged. It is almost universally accepted, without question, even by those who are not members of a particular religious group, that human life is, in some important sense, *sacred*. 'Thou shalt not kill' (Exodus 20:13) is central to every moral code, religious and secular, and to unjustly kill an innocent human being is almost unanimously held to be the most heinous of crimes, even by those who commit that crime. Nonetheless, the first premise of the conservative position can be challenged. Indeed, doing so totally transforms and considerably clarifies the abortion issue.

Singer notes that, 'The weakness of the first premise of the conservative argument is that it relies on our acceptance of the special status of *human* life' (*Practical Ethics*, p. 117). In order to understand why this is a weakness we need to analyse the pivotal term 'human', a term that is too often used in an ambiguous and misleading way, particularly within the abortion debate.

Strictly speaking, the term 'human' simply refers to a member of the species *homo sapiens*. The term 'human' is, however, also used as though it were synonymous with the term 'person'. A *person* is any being, not just a human being, that is conscious, self-conscious, rational, autonomous, curious, able to experience pleasure and pain, able to suffer, has a sense of past and future, a desire to go on living, is capable of relating to others, communicating with others, being concerned for others and so on.

Importantly, Singer and others argue that it is possession of these *personal* qualities, *personhood*, that renders a being worthy of moral consideration rather than it simply being a member of a particular species. Singer refers to these personal qualities as *morally relevant characteristics*.

Most human beings, being also fully fledged persons, have a high degree of morally relevant characteristics and are, therefore, worthy of the highest degree of moral consideration. A stone, on the other hand, lacking any personhood other than what might be projected onto it by the imagination of a person, has no morally relevant characteristics. It is not therefore possible to act immorally towards a stone. If I smash your pet stone with a sledgehammer, it is you that I offend, not the stone.

To assume that a being has moral relevance simply by virtue of being a member of a particular species is misguided. To assume that a member of one species has *more* or *less* moral relevance than a member of another species, simply because it is a member of that species, is what Singer calls *speciesism*. Speciesism is little different from *racism*, the assumption that a human person of one race, simply by virtue of being a member of that race, is more or less valuable and morally significant than a human person of another race.

Speciesism with regard to human beings is often expressed through the religious doctrine, 'Human life is sacred and should never be killed.' But if human life is sacred, why is not *all* life sacred? Why the bias towards humans? If all life were sacred then we would not only act immorally every time we swatted a fly or ate a chicken, actions that are held by some to be immoral, but also every time we ate a carrot, applied an antiseptic or squirted germ killer down the toilet, actions which are not seriously held by anyone to be immoral.

You may have already worked out that interrogating the term 'human', and thereby introducing the concepts of *personhood*, *morally relevant characteristics* and *speciesism*, places the abortion debate on a whole new footing. These concepts also have huge bearing on the animal rights debate, which we shall consider in due course.

In light of our new understanding, the first premise of the conservative argument – 'It is wrong to kill an innocent human being' – is revealed as false. As argued, it is not wrong to kill anything simply by virtue of its being a member of a species. The conservative will of course reply that by human being they mean human person, in which case the second premise of their argument becomes false because a foetus is not a person. A foetus is not rational, self-conscious, autonomous, curious, communicative, planning its future or pondering its past.

Even if we allow that due to its *advanced* level of physical and possibly mental development, a foetus *above* a certain number of weeks of gestation has some degree of personhood and therefore moral relevance, this only seems to reinforce the view that due to its *lack* of physical and mental development, a foetus *below* a certain number of weeks of gestation has no personhood and therefore no moral relevance.

The conclusion to the conservative argument is overturned. It is not wrong to kill a human foetus, certainly *below* a certain number of weeks of gestation. Those legal systems that draw the line for legal abortion at or around twenty-four weeks, longer if the life of the fully fledged *person* carrying the foetus is threatened, would appear to have it just about right, to be legislating with good common sense and due moral consideration.

Singer, a staunch advocate of animal rights, argues that if the prejudice of speciesism and the hollowness of the claim that human life is sacred are to be avoided, the life of a human foetus has to be valued on the *same scale* as the lives of other beings that are not members of our species. The value or lack of value of the life of a human foetus has to be weighed against the value or lack of value of the lives of, for example, a prawn, a fish, a chicken, a cow, a pig, a monkey and so on.

> For on any fair comparison of morally relevant characteristics, like rationality, self-consciousness, awareness, autonomy, pleasure and pain, and so on, the calf, the pig and the much derided chicken come out well ahead of the fetus at any stage of pregnancy – while if we take the comparison with a fetus of less than three months, a fish, or even a prawn would show more signs of consciousness.
>
> *Practical Ethics*, p. 118

The so-called *pro-life* lobby is misnamed, in that it does not have an impartial concern for all life but only a biased concern for the lives of members of its own human species. The majority of pro-life activists, not being vegetarians, are hypocrites for happily tucking into beef steaks and roast chicken while campaigning to preserve the lives of human foetuses. A few very confused pro-life militants have even murdered doctors who conducted abortions.

Confronted by those arguments that centre around the human/person distinction, conservatives are sometimes tempted to shift ground somewhat in order to try and shore up their position. They argue that it is wrong to kill a *potential* human being and that there is no doubt the foetus is a potential human being, whether human being is taken to mean instance of *homo sapiens* or person. The second premise is undeniable, the foetus is a potential human person, but this indubitable second premise is gained only by weakening the *original* conservative first premise that it is wrong to kill an innocent human being.

To insist that something is a *potential* x is to admit that it is not an *actual* x, and generally a potential x does not have the rights of an actual x. A potential president, for example, does not enjoy all the rights and privileges of an actual president. A potential person, by definition, *lacks* the morally relevant characteristics of self-consciousness, autonomy and so on that, if it possessed them, would immediately render it an actual person with a right to life.

In so far as the *basis* of the so-called *basic human rights* of actual persons is the possession of morally relevant characteristics, a potential person has no basic human rights because it has no morally relevant characteristics.

The Animal Rights Issue

Towards a Notion of Animal Rights

The debate regarding how we ought to treat non-human animals is as old as philosophy itself. The ancient Greek, pre-Socratic philosopher and mathematician Pythagoras argued that non-human animals should be treated with respect because they contain the reincarnated souls of humans. This, of course, is really only an argument in favour of respecting humans and begs the question: how should animals be treated supposing they do not contain the reincarnated souls of humans? At least Pythagoras was willing to grant that animals were more than automata, which was more than some later philosophers were prepared to do.

In his *Great Chain of Being* that has God at the top and non-precious rocks at the bottom, Aristotle placed animals well below humans in terms of importance. Animals, he held, have no real interests of their own, their behaviour being determined by nature and instinct rather than by their own reason. Some animals, he acknowledged, possess a semblance of reason, but genuine reason is unique to humans.

For Aristotle, the best, most exclusive definition of 'man' is 'rational animal' because human beings are the only beings that are both animals and rational. Aristotle, like most thinkers who followed him down through the centuries, particularly in the Christian tradition, judged an animal's worth and moral standing not by its *sentience*, its *ability* to perceive and feel, but by its *inability* to reason as humans do.

Aristotle's colleague Theophrastus, however, held that it is unjust to kill animals because they *can* reason, exhibit intelligent behaviour and often share psychological qualities with humans. He was one of the earliest known advocates of abstinence from eating meat on moral grounds; an animal rights supporter way ahead of his time given that views similar to his were not at all widely held until quite recently. Unfortunately, certainly for animals, it was the Aristotelian view that prevailed.

Perhaps the most impoverished view of animals and their worth is found in the philosophy of the French rationalist René Descartes. A great and pioneering thinker in many ways, Descartes tended, nonetheless, to be a man who refused to allow common sense and empirical observation to undermine a neat metaphysical theory. In holding that mind and matter are entirely separate (dualism), and that mind is God's unique gift to humankind, Descartes argues that animals, as part and parcel of a physical universe that is entirely mechanistic in its nature, are merely sophisticated *automata* wholly lacking consciousness and subjectivity.

In opposition to Descartes, the English empiricist philosopher John Locke held the more sensible view that animals can at least feel and so suffer and that therefore cruelty towards them on the part of humans is immoral. Like most thinkers of his time, however, Locke was primarily concerned with how cruelty towards an animal reflects upon the human perpetrator rather than with the welfare of the animal itself.

Like Kant after him, Locke held that wanton cruelty towards animals hardens a person's heart and deadens his feelings of sympathy, inclining him to act maliciously towards other humans. Locke says:

> One thing I have frequently observed in children, that, when they have got possession of any poor creature, they are apt to use it ill; they often torment and treat very roughly young birds, butterflies, and such other poor animals, which fall into their hands, and that with a seeming kind of pleasure. This, I think, should be watched in them; and if they incline to any such cruelty, they should be taught the contrary usage; for the custom of tormenting and killing of beasts will, by degrees, harden their minds even towards men; and they who delight in the suffering and destruction of inferior creatures, will not be apt to be very compassionate or benign to those of their own kind.
>
> *Some Thoughts Concerning Education*, 116, p. 85

It is certainly the case, as any psychologist will tell you, that those psychopaths who go on to commit violent crimes against humans – serial killers and rapists and so on – often begin as children and teenagers by torturing and wantonly killing animals. Do they do this because they have psychopathic tendencies, or do they acquire psychopathic tendencies by doing this?

Whatever the precise answer, it seems reasonable to suppose that practising cruelty on animals as a youngster is, as Locke argues, likely to deepen an individual's taste for cruelty towards animals *and* humans as an adult. Every educational effort should be made, therefore, to extinguish the childish habit of cruelty towards animals as early as possible, perhaps by somehow redirecting the child's energies and curiosity towards caring for animals.

The sentiment that wanton cruelty towards animals is bad for both man and beast began to find some expression in law during the seventeenth century. In Ireland, in 1635, a law was passed to prevent pulling wool off sheep and ploughing by the tail.

A simple plough that did not require a harness was often attached to a horse's tail, inflicting great suffering on the poor beast. The law was primarily an expression of Protestant contempt for the barbaric habits of the Gaelic Irish, with the main consequence being a handsome fee for the Protestant collector of fines rather than any significant prevention of the practice. Nonetheless, a legal *precedent* was set for enshrining animal protection in law.

In 1654 the English government under Oliver Cromwell introduced animal protection laws that emphasized the Puritan view that man's dominion over animals, as granted in the Bible (Genesis 1:26), meant responsible *stewardship*, not irresponsible *ownership*.

Cromwell despised blood sports, a wide variety of vile practices that involve torturing, injuring and killing animals for the sordid entertainment of spectators: dog fighting, cockfighting, bull fighting, bear baiting and so on. Cromwell was not, however, so much concerned with the plight of the animals abused as with preventing the idleness, drunkenness and gambling that surrounded these practices. The Puritans did not like people having fun, bloodstained or otherwise.

In France, in the eighteenth century, the great philosophical polemicist Voltaire railed against the practice of dissecting live dogs for medical research, arguing that the practice was immoral because dogs and similar animals are not automata, as Descartes claimed, but as sentient as any human being.

This was the start of a long and heated debate which still rages regarding the extent to which *vivisection* and other scientific experimentation using animals is morally acceptable: not at all, or on certain animals under certain regulated conditions for certain highly beneficial purposes? Beneficial, that is, to humans, not to the animals experimented on.

Consider, for example, the likely moral difference between using monkeys for medical research into cures for deadly diseases, and so-called *Dieselgate*: Volkswagen locking monkeys in small chambers and exposing them to diesel exhaust. Incidentally, Volkswagen also suppressed their findings that diesel was a far more harmful pollutant than they hoped it would be. So, the monkeys really did suffer for nothing given that human lives were lost as a result of the cover-up, rather than saved, as they could have been, as a result of the research.

Around the same time as Voltaire, the Father of the French Revolution Jean-Jacques Rousseau also argued for the better treatment of animals on the grounds that their sentience makes them worthy of moral consideration. Rousseau held that people have certain inalienable *natural rights* by virtue of being people, by virtue of being sentient, rational and so on. Recall Singer's key notion of *morally relevant characteristics*.

Rousseau argues that although animals lack liberty, intelligence and an understanding of natural law, they are nonetheless very similar to human persons in their nature and as such have certain inalienable natural rights that ought to be respected by human persons. Rousseau was one of the first philosophers to argue that animals have moral rights and that, therefore, human persons have certain moral duties towards them based on those rights, rather than duties towards them based on other considerations, the will of God for example. As Rousseau says in his *Discourse on Inequality* (1755):

> By this method also we put an end to the time-honoured disputes concerning the participation of animals in natural law: for it is clear that, being destitute of intelligence and liberty, they cannot recognise that law; as they partake, however, in some measure of our nature, in consequence of the sensibility with which they are endowed, they ought to partake of natural right; so that mankind is subjected to a kind of obligation even toward the brutes. It appears,

in fact, that if I am bound to do no injury to my fellow-creatures, this is less because they are rational than because they are sentient beings: and this quality, being common both to men and beasts, ought to entitle the latter at least to the privilege of not being wantonly ill-treated by the former.

Discourse on Inequality, Preface, p. 55

The Question Is: Can They Suffer?

In his *An Introduction to the Principles of Morals and Legislation*, written just five years after Rousseau published his *Discourse on Inequality*, Bentham, as we have seen, dismissed any notion of natural rights and duties as fundamental principles existing outside or prior to the establishment of a civil society. Hence, he disagrees with Rousseau that animals 'partake of natural right'. Bentham nonetheless agrees with Rousseau that animals are worthy of moral consideration, not on account of their rationality, which is often limited or lacking, but on account of their sentience. He argues that at least some of the moral rights that are granted to humans on the basis of the principle of *utility* should be extended to animals as well.

Like humans, animals are capable of suffering, and therefore have an interest in not suffering that ought to be respected. There is no reasonable justification for taking human suffering into moral consideration while refusing to take animal suffering into moral consideration. To do so is what has come to be known as *speciesism*, prejudicial bias towards one's own species, which, as said, is on a par with racism. Bentham's utilitarian position regarding the moral status of animals is well summed up in this famous passage, the last sentence of which is probably the best-known comment on animal rights ever uttered by anyone:

The French have already discovered that the blackness of the skin is no reason why a human being should be abandoned without redress to the caprice of a tormentor. It may come one day to be recognised, that the number of legs, the villosity [hairiness] of the skin, or the termination of the *os sacrum* [possession of a tail], are reasons equally insufficient for abandoning a sensitive creature to the same fate. What else is it that should trace the insuperable line? Is it the faculty of reason, or, perhaps, the faculty of discourse? But a full-grown horse or dog is beyond comparison a more rational, as well as a more conversable animal, than an infant of a day, of a week, or even a month, old. But suppose the case were otherwise, what would it avail? The question is not, Can they *reason*? nor, Can they *talk*? but, Can they *suffer*?

An Introduction to the Principles of Morals and Legislation, p. 311

To cause an animal to suffer, or to fail to reduce its suffering where possible, is to add to the sum total of pain in the world and to detract from the sum total of pleasure, which, in utilitarian terms, is immoral. It can, however, be argued that the pleasure of those who enjoy causing animals to suffer has to be set against the pain of the suffering animal.

To get out of this difficulty Bentham could argue that the intense mental and physical agony of, for example, a bear baited by dogs for the entertainment of an audience will always outweigh the pleasure of the audience, but for Bentham that may depend on the size of the audience.

Recall that Bentham considers pleasure only *quantitatively* not *qualitatively.* If push-pin has the same value as poetry then bear baiting has the same value as Beethoven. Fortunately, Mill's more sophisticated view that there are *qualitative* differences between pleasures, that there are higher and lower pleasures, does provide a basis for arguing that the pleasure of those who enjoy blood sports is so *low* as to be thoroughly base and sordid.

Arguably, blood sporting is the sick pleasure of brutes and ignoramuses who, if they were more educated, civilized and refined, would not find blood sports pleasurable. Blood sporting, which includes hunting animals for the sole enjoyment of killing them, is a squalid pleasure that should never be weighed against the real pain of an animal, any more than the sick pleasure of a rapist should be weighed against the suffering of his victim.

Many utilitarians do allow that no more suffering than is absolutely necessary can be caused to an animal if that suffering is an unavoidable consequence of research that is of great utility to humankind in terms of promoting the greatest happiness. The lower pleasure of, for example, wearing cosmetics that have been perfected by causing animals to suffer in laboratories does not justify the suffering. On the other hand, the higher pleasure generated for many people by, for example, a life-saving cancer drug that has been perfected by causing animals to suffer in laboratories does justify the suffering.

Opponents of this view argue that no animal should ever be made to suffer in the name of medical research, however great the resulting medical advances are. These opponents often also hold the unsustainable and certainly impractical view that *all* animals should be granted the same moral rights as human beings. That it is morally wrong, for example, to counter a plague of rats with rat poison or a swarm of crop-devouring locusts with pesticide.

Others allow that it is acceptable for so-called *lower* animals, insects, mice and so on, to suffer in the name of medical research if there is no viable alternative to experimenting with living creatures, but that so-called *higher* animals, dogs, apes and so on, should never be permitted to suffer in the name of medical research, however great the resulting medical advances are.

Only a Nazi would consider causing a new-born human baby to suffer in the name of medical research, so why do we cause various non-human primates, with far more morally relevant characteristics than new-born human babies, to suffer in the name of medical research? If moral considerations are overriding, then the argument that using non-human primates is the *only* way to conduct the research does not justify the research.

Of course, those who morally object to the use of higher animals in medical research must accept that medical science will not be able to go on offering them and their loved ones so many new miracle cures if experiments using higher animals cease. They will likely respond to this point by insisting that higher animals need never be used in medical research, that using them is invariably laziness or stupidity or wanton cruelty on the part of scientists, that there are always viable research alternatives. Unfortunately, that this is the case is highly improbable.

In arguing that animals should not be made to suffer unnecessarily, most utilitarians do not thereby argue that animals should not be killed for the purpose of eating them. To kill an animal quickly and painlessly is not to make it suffer, and even if an entirely painless death is impossible, the death an animal receives at the hands of a responsible and competent butcher is generally far quicker and far less painful than the lingering death it would eventually receive at the hands of nature. Bentham again:

> If the being eaten were all, there is very good reason why we should be suffered to eat such of them as we like to eat: we are the better for it, and they are never the worse. They have none of those long-protracted anticipations of future misery which we have. The death they suffer in our hands commonly is, and always may be, a speedier, and by that means a less painful one, than that which would await them in the inevitable course of nature. If the being killed were all, there is very good reason why we should be suffered to kill such as molest us: we should be the worse for their living, and they are never the worse for being dead. But is there any reason why we should be suffered to torment them? Not any that I can see.
>
> *An Introduction to the Principles of Morals and Legislation*, p. 311

Bentham clearly holds that eating meat is not in itself morally wrong, although others will argue that some animals, pigs perhaps, have sufficient morally relevant characteristics, sufficient *personhood*, to make killing them and consuming their flesh reprehensible however painlessly they are slaughtered. We do not excuse a murderer for making a *clean* kill of another human being and in the minds of some all meat production is murder.

On the subject of animal slaughter, the modern method is to stun the animal into unconsciousness with electricity, gas or captive bolt pistol before subjecting it to exsanguination by cutting its throat or into its heart. Stunning was introduced because it is kinder to the animal than proceeding directly to exsanguination, although animal rights campaigners note that stunning methods are not always as efficient or well applied as they should be. In The Smiths' cheerful little ditty 'Meat is Murder', Morrissey asks us if we know how animals die, emotively insisting that smilingly carving a calf or festively slicing a turkey are both murder.

If we take Bentham's point that what counts morally is the *suffering* of an animal, then immorality attaches not to eating meat as such but rather to the shoddy ways in which many animals are kept before they are turned into meat. People are vegetarians for a variety of reasons: health, taste, fastidiousness, religion, concern about the impact on the environment of rearing so many animals for their flesh and so on. Only some vegetarians believe that eating meat is, in itself, immoral. Many do not object to people eating meat as such, but rather to *factory farming methods*.

The harrowing details of factory farming are extensive, you can look them up for yourself if you want to, but the overriding feature of the factory farming of poultry, pigs and cattle is very high *stocking densities* for the purpose of maximizing efficiency and profit. Animals that are cooped up or penned in, so that their bodily movement is severely restricted, are unable to indulge their *natural behaviours*: foraging by pecking and scratching in the case of chickens for example, rooting with the snout in the case of pigs for example.

Many animal rights campaigners and enlightened legislators argue that an animal suffers ill health and stress when it is unable to indulge its natural behaviours, and this view seems to be supported by the empirical evidence of assessments of the health of intensively farmed animals as compared with the health of farm animals kept in more natural conditions. Not least, intensively farmed animals are more prone to disease and have to be pumped with antibiotics and other drugs to compensate. These pharmaceutically drenched animals are then, of course, consumed by humans.

Defenders of factory farming, usually those with vested interests, tend to argue that animals do not miss what they have never had and are not sufficiently intelligent to be bothered about the conditions under which they are kept. They also argue that consumers receive the 'benefit' of cheap meat, albeit substandard. There seems to be in all this a tacit admission that the farm animals in their care are suffering, but that this does not matter because they are incapable of consciously reflecting on that suffering. They seek to downplay the suffering of the farm animals in their care by appealing to the animals' limited ability to reason rather than to their clear capacity to feel.

Non-human Animal Persons

Some of the main features of the modern animal rights debate were revealed when we considered abortion. We saw that the key question in the abortion debate concerns whether or not a human foetus possesses the morally relevant characteristics that render it a *person* worthy of moral consideration. The key question in the animal rights debate is essentially the same: do non-human animals have morally relevant characteristics that render them *persons* worthy of moral consideration?

The short answer is that some non-human animals certainly do. A good many non-human animals possess morally relevant characteristics to a degree far greater than a well-developed human foetus or even a new-born baby, and some non-human animals possess morally relevant characteristics to a degree more than sufficient to render them full-blown persons.

In defining the term 'person' as referring not only to a member of the species *homo sapiens* but to any being that is rational, self-conscious, autonomous, curious and so on, it is clear that certain non-human animals are persons and should be fully respected as such. Not to respect them as such, while rightly respecting human persons, is simply speciesism.

> Hence we should reject the doctrine [speciesism] that places members of our species above the lives of members of other species. Some members of other species are persons: some members of our own species are not . . . So it seems that killing, say, a chimpanzee [thousands are killed by humans annually] is worse than killing a gravely defective human who is not a person.
>
> *Practical Ethics*, p. 97

Cognitively, emotionally and socially, highly sophisticated primates, such as chimps and bonobos, are undoubtedly persons. Also dolphins and whales. Other animals that are remarkably well endowed with personal qualities are corvids, octopi, pigs, dogs and cats.

Singer admits that in the case of pigs, dogs and cats it is difficult to say for definite that these animals are persons. We do not ultimately know and will probably never know what their inner life is truly like, and we must always be wary of *anthropomorphism*. On the common-sense face of it, however, these animals appear to be so well endowed with personal characteristics that we should, as Singer recommends, give them the benefit of the doubt.

What owner of a cat, dog or horse doubts for a moment that these very responsive, behaviourally rich, even affectionate creatures are persons, at least when that owner understands that 'person' is a term that can apply to non-human animals? Recall Bentham's delightful but nonetheless very sensible point that a full-grown horse is beyond comparison a more rational and more conversable animal than a human infant of even a month old – a thoroughly inept creature with very undeveloped capacities, beyond mewling and puking, that is nevertheless generally accepted as being a full-blown person.

Arguably, *none* of the above-mentioned animals, by virtue of their definite or highly probable personhood, should be made to suffer for *any* reason, or be killed for *any* reason, other than to put them out of extreme misery. It is certainly extremely morally inconsistent of people who endorse *human rights* to fail to endorse the moral rights of higher animals.

Now, here am I endorsing the moral rights of higher animals while looking forward to a bacon sandwich for my lunch, which surely makes me something of a hypocrite, a preacher of what I do not practise. I would like to put it down to weakness of will. I know the better course of action yet I do not follow it because I relish bacon so much, but really the truth is that I am, like most people, simply not as concerned about the life of pigs and other higher animals as I should be. Although I do care, without actively campaigning for it, about their welfare while they are alive.

Does the fact that I eat bacon make me as unspeakable as those people I earlier described as brutes and ignoramus who injure and kill animals for the sheer pleasure of doing so? I think not, as surely killing a decently reared farm animal painlessly – if animals can be killed painlessly – for the purpose of eating it is nowhere near as bad as causing an animal to suffer and die for a moronic, sadistic and entirely unnecessary thrill.

An animal, I often opine, should never be killed for pleasure or entertainment. But isn't killing an animal to eat it killing it for pleasure rather than out of necessity, given that many other types of food besides meat are available in the developed world where I am fortunate enough to reside?

The debate continues, and I am certainly aware that there are many *specific* issues within the huge area of animal rights that it has been beyond the scope of this chapter to explore. For example, the deliberate breeding of dogs with genetically based respiratory problems because their cuteness pleases human vanity, or the criminal hunting of elephants for ivory, or the controversial practice of allowing sad, supercilious, super-rich, cowardly creeps to trophy hunt a controlled amount of endangered mammals because the big fees they pay help fund conservation.

One notorious example of the modern big-game hunter is the Bible-quoting creationist from Texas who is shooting and mounting the African 'big five' in order to overcome feelings of inadequacy instilled in him by a bullying father, also a big-game hunter. He believes that shooting big game puts him closer to Daddy and God while also disproving the theory of evolution. The argument goes that when you shoot a hippo or a lion for fun and self-glorification it is impossible to believe that they *evolved* and obvious that God put them on earth to be killed for human entertainment.

This individual has been filmed weeping with a disturbing mixture of conceit and pity over the carcass of a dead male lion he has just shot for pleasure, a beast he clearly sees as more magnificent dead than alive. Good person though you are, you may find yourself hoping that on his next killing binge he misses his prey by about 180 degrees. His next target is a rhino.

Anyway, it is hoped that all such specific, emotive, animal rights issues can be clarified by applying the various concepts we have established – sentience, suffering, morally relevant characteristics, personhood, speciesism and so on. They are all, without doubt, useful notions to stick in your by now overflowing ethical toolkit.

5
CONCLUDING REMARKS
How to Be Good

So, how to be good then, *morally* good that is. Well, as we have seen, you will never be a good *thing*, good in the way that a chair *is* a chair, shot through with goodness like a stick of Blackpool rock is shot through with the legend 'Blackpool Rock'. You will never be so saturated in incorruptible goodness that when you die your saintly corpse will not rot, as though pickled and preserved in goodness. Goodness is just not that sort of thing. In fact, it is not a *thing* at all. You cannot bottle it.

Goodness is about behaviour and attitude, largely your conduct and approach towards other people. It is something that you do and have to keep on doing all the time in order to be a good person. It is possible to have a *good character*, but to have a good character is not to be a good *thing*, but rather to be so in the habit of *doing* good and *avoiding* bad that it has become second nature to you.

It is, it seems, *possible* to be morally good, to genuinely *choose* to act morally as opposed to immorally. If *causal determinism* were true it would be impossible to make genuine choices or to be responsible for anything, but it appears that causal determinism is not the case as far as human behaviour is concerned, and certainly it has not been proven to be the case.

It is counter-intuitive to insist that we never make genuine choices and, indeed, the entire human world functions, and must function, on the sensible assumption that we do make genuine choices, including moral choices. 'We *know* our will is free, and *there's* an end on't' (Samuel Johnson in James Boswell, *Life of Johnson*, p. 411).

It is also, it seems, possible to be morally good, to act in a genuinely altruistic way, as opposed to always acting in your own self-interest. Like the notion of causal determinism, the notion of *psychological egoism* breaks down under scrutiny. Wanting to help others, for example, does not have to be reduced to really wanting to help yourself by helping them.

If people get satisfaction from helping others then there surely has to be something *intrinsically* good about doing so. A mother nurses a sick child because she cares about the child, not because she gets some sort of weird, selfish satisfaction out of helping the child that is really all about herself and nothing to do with the child.

With those barriers to the very possibility of being morally good out of the way, you can get on with acquiring knowledge about what is actually involved in being good and bad. That is, take on board the various *normative* theories that seek to distinguish right from wrong, then try to act as they advise in your everyday life and dealings with others. Apart from a few *moral dilemmas* you might find yourself confronted with from time to time, where it is difficult to know which course of action to take for the best, doing the right thing is not exactly rocket science.

Most of the time what you *ought* to do in a situation is pretty darned obvious. It is often only *not wanting* to do what ought to be done in a situation that leads a person to *pretend* that they did not realize what the right course of action was. Having said that, the great normative moral theories do sometimes conflict with each other about what is good and right and what is bad and wrong, but actually most of the time they agree, even if they arrive at what ought to be done by somewhat different paths.

As a rule of thumb you can follow the *golden rule* of treating others as you want them to treat you, but remember people have different wants, and you are unlikely to want everyone to treat you how they want to be treated. Most people have moderate wants, a little cash, a little adventure, a little love and affection, but some people have very strange and destructive wants. If you happen to want, for example, to have pain and humiliation inflicted on you, that probably does not make it ok for you to inflict pain and humiliation on others.

So why not opt for that more sophisticated moral principle that looks a bit like the golden rule but is not. Why not follow Kant's highly rational and civilized *categorical imperative* and 'act only on that maxim through which you can at the same time will that it should become a universal law' (*Groundwork*, p. 84). Living according to the categorical imperative will make you a good person. You will not steal or lie or make false promises because these practices cannot be universalized without contradiction.

Moreover, you will not treat others as a *mere* means to your own ends but always respect them as ends in themselves, as free rational beings with their own goals. Murder, rape, slavery, exploitation, all these vices are ruled out by the categorical imperative. All is respect and consent in Kant's *kingdom of ends*, an ideal world you will be helping to bring about by living in accordance with the categorical imperative.

There is, of course, that tricky problem of the supposed right to lie from altruistic motives. If you are living entirely true to the categorical imperative then you must never lie, even if the Nazis are at your door asking after the man you just hid under your floorboards. You could try saying nothing or try to throw them off the scent without lying as Saint Athanasius did with the Roman soldiers, but these ploys may well not work.

What can I say? Well, although it goes against Kant's whole moral philosophy to suggest that you should lie to get yourself out of a difficulty, that you should ever adopt non-universalizable maxims, I say, on such rare occasions, tell the lie, because you would be a complete moral ass if you told the truth.

I am saying, in effect, that on those occasions where you really, really need to tell a white lie, to save a life or something, put the categorical imperative away in your ethical toolkit and take out your utilitarian, multipurpose sonic screwdriver instead. I recognize that this recommendation is not entirely logical but it does nonetheless have a certain practical wisdom about it.

That is how most of us roll anyway, a pinch of categorical imperative here, a smattering of utilitarianism there. You just have to be careful that you do not flip from one to the other just because it suits your selfish purposes and your efforts to put a positive spin on your choices.

I can hear Kant spinning in his grave all the way over there in Konigsberg, doubtless asking by what *new* rational principle one would decide when it was ok to flip from *deontological* principles to *consequentialist* principles. I have no answer to that, other than that there seems to be value in both deontological and consequentialist ethics and it is a shame that you cannot somehow follow both by turns.

Anyway, you will not go far wrong if all your actions aim at promoting the greatest happiness for the greatest number. It is generally not difficult to recognize which actions are socially constructive.

Smiling at a stranger, they say, spreads a great deal of good will and happiness, although be careful not to get your face smashed in. Some strangers can be very funny about strangers smiling at them. Give to charities that are helping people to help themselves and never drop litter or fly-tip because there is absolutely no excuse for such filthy, antisocial, un-utilitarian behaviour.

I absolutely cannot understand why people drop litter. Murder often has more justification. It surely cannot be explained by laziness with regard to finding a bin, so perhaps it has to be explained as motivated by spitefulness, an anarchic desire to hit back at society, or perhaps even some weirdly selfish litter-dropping sexual fetish.

That litter louts do not like waste material is clearly revealed by the fact that they are so keen to discard it, yet they are quite happy for it to clog every street, lane, hedgerow, beach and river where it is a curse to wildlife and deeply offensive to everyone except other litter louts. Litter, especially plastic litter, is the new scum of the earth, dropped by scum of the earth.

Act utilitarianism, where you calculate the likely consequences of your actions on an *act by act* basis, is likely to get you into trouble morally. If Kantian ethics is inflexible then utilitarianism can lack a sense of *justice*. 'I think I will make a human bridge of this old man and then all these people can trample across him to safety.' It just isn't fair.

If you are going to be a good utilitarian, and I highly recommend it, then you probably need to be a *rule utilitarian* who focuses on the utility of rules prescribing *types* of action. That way you will not be tempted to use old men as human bridges or kill the proverbial innocent child in order to somehow save a whole city's worth of people, because *as a rule* using individuals in these ways does not promote the greatest happiness. Following rule utilitarianism is good because it protects vulnerable individuals and minorities from the so-called tyranny of the majority. Cruder forms of utilitarianism do not.

You can also pick and choose from a variety of *variants* of utilitarianism. *Preference utilitarianism*, for example, recommends that you do not try to satisfy *all* of your preferences – you will inevitably be disappointed if you do – but rather settle for satisfying only *some* of your preferences. Go in for *satisficing* rather than *optimizing*, that way you are more likely to make other people happy by allowing them to satisfy at least some of *their* preferences.

A good person is not one who allows others to walk all over him or her, but he nonetheless recognizes the constant need for *compromise*, for give and take, for negotiating the best outcome all round given that real-life circumstances almost never allow everyone to get everything they want. One of the most morally constructive things to be in this life is a good and honest diplomat.

As to the *idealistic utilitarianism* of G. E. Moore, there is surely a lot of truth in his claim that intrinsic value belongs to friendship and aesthetic experience, while intrinsic disvalue belongs to disdain for beauty and to enjoyment of whatever is ugly, sordid and ignoble, dropping litter for example. The former should always be promoted, the latter always discouraged.

A good person recognizes that there is nothing more valuable in life than the company and support of friends and family on the one hand and aesthetic experience on the other: art, literature, philosophy, film, music, sport, good food, craftsmanship, creativity, a stroll on the beach, a hike in the mountains; you name it, whatever counts as a higher pleasure and satisfies the higher faculties. Interestingly, most of these things are either free or relatively cheap. A good person sees the sense in that old adage, 'The best things in life are free.'

Respect other people as ends in themselves, try to make sure your actions promote the greatest happiness for the greatest number, or at least do not add to the sum total of pain and misery in the world, and strive to develop your *character* so that on all fronts it strikes the *golden mean* of *moderation in all things*. This requires the wisdom of knowing yourself, understanding your personal strengths and weaknesses. Strive to overcome your weaknesses and play to your strengths, without getting carried away and succumbing to *hubris*.

Consciously strive to overcome your natural timidity, for example, which could lead you to shy away from good opportunities or, worse, into acts of cowardice. At the other extreme, seek to control your over-confidence and quick temper before you rush rashly towards danger and possible destruction.

Wisdom requires an honest and sensible assessment of your life circumstances. Ask yourself, what, for me, for example, constitutes overindulgence, moderation and insensitivity, or profligacy, generosity and meanness. One person's overindulgence is another person's moderation, one person's generosity is another person's profligacy. It all depends on your stamina and resources.

Remember that being good is often not the same as being nice. A nice person who is overflowing with sympathy for others and gives too much of his wealth away may actually be a less moral person than the person who is less charitable but more self-reliant such that he never becomes a charity case himself.

There is much to be said in favour of good, old-fashioned values like self-reliance, self-respect, self-discipline, courage, proper pride, stoicism, dignity and honour, especially in a modern world that lays too much emphasis on pity, self-pity, emotional excess, excusing weakness, blaming others, wastefulness and so on. In short, strive to be a great and magnanimous soul. Cry sparingly like tough old Ahab so that your tears really count for something. Life is tough and it is surely impossible to be a good person unless you are also in your own way an emotionally strong person. Forbearance is a virtue as great as it is underrated.

You do not have to become a Buddhist to be a good person but there is a lot to learn from Buddhism about the right and best way to live. The golden mean of Aristotle and the *middle way* of the Buddha have much in common and a person could do far worse in life than pin the *eightfold path* to his wall and broadly aspire to live by it: realism, commitment, tact, respect, decency, enthusiasm, mindfulness, concentration.

It is morally good to be true to what you are, and what you are is a free, self-determining being responsible for your choices. *Authenticity* involves taking full responsibility for all your choices. Authenticity even involves embracing every new situation as though you chose it, even if you did not choose it.

If you are authentic, rather than bemoaning your lot while pathetically wishing you were someone else somewhere else, you will always immediately accept your *being-in-situation* by striving to make the most of difficult circumstances and by dealing resolutely with every eventuality. The authentic person is a *realist*, always ready for whatever life throws at him. A person seldom helps himself or others by being an idle, unrealistic dreamer or complainer.

To be authentic is to resist *regret* because to regret is to wish you were other than you are today by wishing your past were other than it is. Rather than regret past actions, view them as a learning experience that made you stronger and wiser. Keep in mind that although it is not possible to change the past as such, it is possible to redefine the meaning of past experiences by giving them a positive outcome.

To be authentic is, above all, to resist *bad faith*. To be in bad faith is to be *inauthentic*. A person in bad faith refuses, in various ways, to take responsibility for who they are and for what they do. At its worst, bad faith leads to the *banality of evil*, to ordinary people, who would not instigate atrocities if left to their own devices, aiding and abetting atrocities by unquestioningly obeying instructions, then feebly refusing to take any responsibility for their complicity on the grounds that they were simply following orders.

Bad faith is refusing to recognize that following orders is *choosing* to follow orders. Bad faith is treating yourself as though you are a *thing* without responsibilities, a mere object acted upon, rather than a conscious, willing being that acts upon the world in accordance with its choices, many of which are *moral* choices. 'It is the drifting icebergs setting with any current anywhere, that wreck the ships' (Charles Dickens, *Hard Times*, p. 175).

Another possible barrier to the very possibility of being good is *moral subjectivism*, the claim that there are no moral facts, the claim that there is no good and bad, no right and wrong, only subjective approval and disapproval of what people do. Moral subjectivism has not been proven, although it seems moral subjectivists are correct about the *naturalistic fallacy*, that there are no moral phenomena, only moral interpretations of phenomena. This does not mean, however, that there is no right and wrong.

Any civilized society will, despite there being various grey areas and dilemmas, always *interpret* some actions as moral and some other actions as immoral, approving of the former because they tend to promote social functioning and disapproving of the latter because they tend to damage social functioning.

'Stealing is wrong', for example, is an expression of disapproval, but it is also shorthand for saying, 'The community cannot function successfully if stealing is allowed to go on unchecked.' Or, 'Stealing upsets people because they feel their valued property is unsafe and because it is *unfair* for a thief simply to take the property someone has worked hard to acquire.'

The moral subjectivist will of course reply 'unfair' here is just an expression of disapproval; it cannot be a *fact* that something is unfair. But, then, is saying it was unfair a goal was incorrectly awarded in a football match also merely an expression of disapproval? Rather, it is a way of expressing that a rule vital to the successful functioning of the game, vital to the very existence of the game, has been ignored, broken and disrespected.

It may be a rule that is made up, as the game of football itself is made up, but it is nonetheless very real in the context of the game. To cheat or make refereeing errors in sport is not simply to do things that spectators *disapprove* of, it is to break or overlook very real rules that *maintain* the very fabric of the game, that *are* the very fabric of the game. Human social life and ethics are no more separable than football and the rules of football.

Like the rules of football, moral rules are very real in so far as they apply to the very real game of everyday human life. Sure, different societies have somewhat different rules, but there are nonetheless reasonable limits to what the rules can be anywhere if anarchy and the collapse of the society are not to ensue. 'Thou, on the whole, shalt not murder.' 'Thou, on the whole, shalt not steal.' 'Thou, on the whole, shalt not lie.'

Recall that *moral relativism* does not imply that anything goes, just as *moral objectivism* need not imply *moral absolutism*. There is no need for a God or anything else metaphysical to make moral rules real. Minimum requirements for social life make moral rules real, real as in necessary, required, indispensable.

Moral subjectivism is, arguably, a hopelessly bookish and pedantic academic position for ivory tower philosophers, who rapidly return to the reality of right and wrong each time they leave their university offices. What philosopher would maintain that the murder of his family was not wrong, simply something he and others disapproved of? Such moral nihilism is no less an absurd and unworkable approach to everyday life as trying to live as a solipsist or causal determinist. That way lies madness.

Anyone involved with real-world ethical issues, where moral theories and decisions literally make the difference between life and death for real people, is likely to be scathing about those academics who trivialize real-world moral concerns by treating ethics as though it were merely a game of chess. Of course, in a free and open society there must be thinkers who are afforded the opportunity to analyse ethics as they see fit and to draw what conclusions they will, just as there must be people who are scathing about them.

Given how people are, the things they tend to want and not want, the things that tend to please them and the things that cause them to suffer, there is always a distinction to be drawn between behaviour that is acceptable and behaviour that is unacceptable. In most everyday situations it is not difficult to decide what is unacceptable, unfair, unjust. Indeed, most of the time it is child's play. Listen to children playing and you will hear the constant voicing of ethical concerns, constant heated argument to establish what is fair and unfair, constant refining of rules to enable play to advance.

In Liverpool, in February 1993, two-year-old James Bulger was abducted and beaten to death by two ten-year-old boys, Robert Thompson and Jon Venables. They threw paint in James's eye while kicking him, stamping on him and throwing bricks at him. They removed all the clothes from the lower half of his body and forcibly retracted his foreskin. They placed batteries into his mouth and possibly into his anus before dropping a 22-pound lump of iron, a railway fishplate, on his head, fracturing his skull in ten places. Finally, they placed his body on a railway track, his head weighted down with rubble, where it was later cut in half by a train.

In November 1993 Thompson and Venables became the youngest convicted murderers in modern English history. Placed in custody until they reached adulthood they were released with new identities in June 2001.

There has been much debate since as to whether or not Thompson and Venables were old enough to know the difference between right and wrong. At their trial it was argued in their defence that because ten-year-olds are not mature and responsible enough to *try* a case for murder as members of a jury, they are not mature and responsible enough to be found guilty of murder.

Against this claim it can be argued that the mental development required to weigh complex and conflicting evidence in a court of law, to judge the credibility of witnesses, to maintain concentration on a lengthy case and so on, is far beyond the very basic mental development required to know that it is wrong, and universally considered to be wrong, to beat a toddler to death, and that doing so will be widely and deeply disapproved of and heavily punished.

It is evident from the police interview tapes that the two boys acted with a clear and sustained intention in abducting James from a shopping centre and taking him to an isolated location four kilometres away. Once there they abused him systematically and understood clearly that they ultimately wanted him to be dead. Both reasonably intelligent and articulate individuals, the boys lied repeatedly and imaginatively to try and cover up their deed, cried without tears when they thought it suited their cause and blamed each other as a last resort before finally confessing with a degree of shame and even embarrassment. All surely clear signs of *mentes reae*.

I do not know what punishment or lack of punishment is suited to ten-year-old murderers, or whether or not justice for all parties concerned was correctly served in this highly emotive and politicised case, but it seems ridiculous psychobabble to argue, as some have done, that the frontal lobes of their ten-year-old brains were not sufficiently developed for them to know what they were doing and that it was very wrong.

The two boys embarked on a sustained undertaking to do a terrible thing seemingly *because* it was a terrible thing to do. It was always clearly far more than a silly game that got out of hand. They could have chosen to turn back from it at any point but did not. That their motives were complex and will remain obscure, not least to themselves, does not imply that they did not *mean* to do what they did.

As psychologists often proclaim, ten-year-olds are, in many ways, sophisticated thinkers. And even if they are not, as some psychologists associated with this case maintain, they are, unless they have severe learning difficulties, more than intelligent and experienced enough to know that it is wrong, bad, not allowed, naughty and nasty to throw bricks at babies.

People who do bad things are often quite unintelligent, yet they usually know full well *why* what they have done is wrong, and not simply that they will be punished for it. Knowing *why* what he has done is wrong, a murderer will lie to a jury that he did not commit the crime. He does not try to convince the jury that murder is not wrong because there are no moral facts, that all the jury needs to do to acquit him is will approval rather than disapproval of his deed.

Exploration of our two chosen moral issues, *abortion* and *animal rights*, revealed the key notion of *morally relevant characteristics*. Some living beings, human and non-human, are worthy of moral consideration by virtue of being *persons* to some extent. If you want to be morally good then you have to understand what *personhood* is and respect it accordingly. Conflating the terms 'human' and 'person' is likely to lead you into *speciesism*, unjustifiably expressing a prejudice in favour of your own species.

Applying these concepts to the abortion issue reveals that because a foetus is not a person, a being with morally relevant characteristics, certainly below a certain number of weeks of gestation, killing a foetus is not morally wrong. As it is likely a foetus above a certain number of weeks of gestation is at least capable of *suffering* then abortions should always be carried out as soon as possible.

Practical considerations relating to her health and well-being mean that no sensible woman requiring an abortion will want to delay having the procedure anyway. Late-term abortions are morally acceptable where the mother's life is threatened because it makes no sense for the minimal personhood of the foetus to outweigh the maximal personhood of the mother.

As to non-human animals, some of them are undoubtedly persons and therefore have *moral rights*. We, therefore, have a *moral duty of care* towards them. Non-human primates, for example, surely have a right not to be killed for any reason at all, other than to put them out of their misery when they are in great pain.

But which animals are to be included in this list alongside non-human primates? Whales and dolphins certainly. Pigs almost certainly, though most of us do not like to admit it because of our unholy craving for bacon, pork sausages and wafer-thin ham. Given its high degree of personhood, is there any animal on earth more abused than the *sus scrofa domesticus*, apart, that is, from humans at the bloody hands of other humans?

As for the humble sheep, although its minimal personhood, limited intelligence and lack of individual characteristics mean that it can easily be replaced by another sheep, we nonetheless have a moral duty, placed upon us by its sentience and capacity to suffer, not to cause it pain or distress when we take its wool or kill it for food.

Regardless of what any particular animal's rights are or are not, a human person who causes any creature to suffer for the sole purpose of his entertainment is not a good person. As the German philosopher Arthur Schopenhauer says in *On the Basis of Morality* (1840), 'Compassion for animals is so intimately associated with goodness of character, it may be confidently asserted that whoever is cruel to animals cannot be a good man' (*On the Basis of Morality*, p. 179).

For his part, pop legend and animal rights activist Paul McCartney is widely held to have said, 'You can judge a man's true character by the way he treats his fellow animals.' There is a lot of truth in this sentiment, given that a person who is wantonly cruel to animals reveals a puerile, pathetic, needless, mean-spirited spitefulness at the bottom of his or her soul.

There are, however, people who are kind to animals who are, nonetheless, morally bad in other ways. Hitler, for example, was an animal lover, a man particularly fond of dogs, and it is a disturbing fact that the Nazis legislated extensively in favour of non-human animal welfare while abusing and exterminating millions of humans. So, being kind to non-human animals is a *necessary* but not a *sufficient* condition of being a morally good person.

Of course, to be good you've got to *want* to be good, and to make some genuine *effort* to live a good life by treating others well and so on. Often, a good person has learnt that it is actually easier and more beneficial overall to be good rather than bad. This leads us back, yet again, to a point that keeps coming up, that goodness has a lot to do with intelligence and badness a lot to do with stupidity. Hitting a pensioner in the face with a hammer for no reason and for no useful purpose is undoubtedly bad but, more than that, it is utterly stupid.

I have often been given the advice, not least by my parents of all people, that I should try to be good, but that if I cannot be good I should be clever. This is meant to mean that if you are going to be bad, make sure you are clever enough not to get caught. But surely, ultimately, the cleverest thing to do, the wisest thing to do, is to be good. After all, it is not so difficult to be good and it is generally very rewarding.

The English dramatist and architect John Vanbrugh once wrote, 'Virtue is its own reward. There's a pleasure in doing good which sufficiently pays itself' (*The Relapse or Virtue in Danger*, Act 5, Scene 2, p. 105). Wise words indeed that would round this book off nicely, except that, in the context of Vanbrugh's Restoration comedy, they are uttered in irony by the naughty but nice Berinthia by way of refusing thanks for her good but probably not *morally good* advice on how to seduce a married woman.

'Thou shalt not covet thy neighbour's wife' (Exodus 20:17), sayeth the Lord. But is coveting thy neighbour's wife (or husband) wrong because God says it is wrong, or does God say it is wrong because it is? The key question is: *why* is it wrong? It cannot be wrong just because God says so. He must surely have a *reason*. Anyway, armed now as you are with your knowledge of the Euthyphro dilemma and all the accumulated moral wisdom of the ages, I leave you to tackle this one for yourself.

BIBLIOGRAPHY

Arendt, Hannah, *Eichmann in Jerusalem: A Report on the Banality of Evil*.
  London: Penguin, 2006.
Aristotle, *Eudemian Ethics*, trans. Brad Inwood. Cambridge: Cambridge
  University Press, 2012.
Aristotle, *Nicomachean Ethics*, trans. J. A. K. Thomson. London: Penguin,
  1976.
Aristotle (Aristotelian School), *Magna Moralia*, in *Aristotle: Metaphysics,
  Books 10–14*, trans. Hugh Tredennick and G. Cyril Armstrong.
  Cambridge, MA: Loeb Classical Library, Harvard University Press, 1989.
Aristotle (Aristotelian School), *On Virtues and Vices* (*De Virtutibus et Vitiis*). In
  The Works of Aristotle, Volume 9. Oxford: Oxford University Press, 1915.
  Digitized by Internet Archive, 2009.
Austen, Jane, *Pride and Prejudice*. London: Penguin, 2003.
Austen, Jane, *Sense and Sensibility*. London: Penguin, 2004.
Ayer, A. J. *Language, Truth and Logic*. London: Penguin, 1990.
Bambrough, Renford, *Moral Scepticism and Moral Knowledge*. London:
  Routledge & Kegan Paul, 1979.
Bentham, Jeremy, *An Introduction to the Principles of Morals and Legislation*.
  New York: Dover Publications, 2007.
Bentham, Jeremy, *The Rationale of Reward*. London: John and H. L. Hunt,
  1825.
Boswell, James, *Life of Johnson*. Oxford: Oxford University Press, 2008.
Butler, Joseph, *Fifteen Sermons and Other Writings on Ethics*, ed. David
  McNaughton. Oxford: Oxford University Press, 2017.
Canadian Government. *Report of the Royal Commission on the Status of
  Women in Canada*, Chair: Florence Bird. Ottawa: Government of Canada
  Publications, 28 September 1970.
Cox, Gary, *The God Confusion*. London: Bloomsbury, 2013.
Crowley, Aleister, *The Book of the Law: Liber Al Vel Legis*. Newburyport, MA:
  Red Wheel/Weiser, 2004.

de Beauvoir, Simone, *The Ethics of Ambiguity*, trans. Bernard Frechtman. New York: Citadel Press, 2000.

Dickens, Charles, *Bleak House*. London: Penguin, 2003.

Dickens, Charles, *Hard Times*. London: Penguin, 2003.

Dickens, Charles, *A Tale of Two Cities*. London: Penguin, 2003.

Diogenes Laërtius, *Lives of the Eminent Philosophers*, trans. Robert Drew Hicks. London: CreateSpace, 2017.

Dostoyevsky, Fyodor, *The Brothers Karamazov*, trans. David McDuff. London: Penguin, 2003.

Frankfurt, Harry G., 'Alternative Possibilities and Moral Responsibility'. *The Journal of Philosophy* 66, no. 23 (4 December 1969): 829–39.

Geach, P. T., *The Virtues*. Cambridge: Cambridge University Press, 1977.

Hare, R. M., *The Language of Morals*. Oxford: Oxford University Press, 1991.

Hobbes, Thomas, *Leviathan*. London: Penguin, 1985.

Horwood, William, *Duncton Wood*. London: Arrow, 1986.

Hume, David, *Enquiries Concerning Human Understanding and Concerning the Principles of Morals*, ed. L. A. Selby-Bigge. Oxford: Oxford University Press, 1975.

Hume, David, *A Treatise of Human Nature*, ed. L. A. Selby-Bigge. Oxford: Oxford University Press, 1978.

Kant, Immanuel, *Critique of Practical Reason*, trans. Mary Gregor. Cambridge: Cambridge University Press, 1997.

Kant, Immanuel, *Critique of Pure Reason*, trans. Norman Kemp Smith. London: Macmillan, 2003.

Kant, Immanuel, *Groundwork of the Metaphysic of Morals*. In *The Moral Law*, trans. H. J. Paton. London: Hutchinson, 1983.

Kant, Immanuel, 'On a Supposed Right to Lie Because of Philanthropic Concerns'. In *Grounding for the Metaphysics of Morals*, trans. James W. Ellington. Indianapolis, IN: Hackett, 1993.

Keats, John, *The Complete Poems*. London: Penguin, 2003.

Kierkegaard, Søren, *The Concept of Anxiety: Kierkegaard's Writings, Vol. 8*. Princeton, NJ: Princeton University Press, 1981.

Locke, John, *An Essay Concerning Human Understanding*. London: Everyman, J. M. Dent, 1993.

Locke, John, *Some Thoughts Concerning Education*. Sioux Falls, SD: NuVision Publications, 2007.

Mackie, J. L., *Ethics: Inventing Right and Wrong*. London: Penguin, 1990.

Melville, Herman, *Moby-Dick*. London: Penguin, 2003.

Merleau-Ponty, Maurice, *Phenomenology of Perception*, trans. Colin Smith. London: Routledge, 2002.

Mill, John Stuart, *John Stuart Mill on Bentham and Coleridge*. New York: Harper & Row, 1962.

Mill, John Stuart, *On Liberty*. In *On Liberty and Other Essays*. Oxford: Oxford University Press, 1998.

Mill, John Stuart, *A System of Logic, Ratiocinative and Inductive*. Cambridge: Cambridge University Press, 2011.

Mill, John Stuart, *Utilitarianism*. In *On Liberty and Other Essays*. Oxford: Oxford University Press, 1998.

Miller, Alexander, *Contemporary Metaethics: An Introduction*. 2nd edn. Cambridge: Polity, 2013.

Moore, G. E., *Principia Ethica*. Cambridge: Cambridge University Press, 1968.

Mounce, H. O., 'Morality and Religion', in *Philosophy of Religion: A Guide to the Subject*, ed. Brian Davies. London: Mowbray, 1998.

Nesbitt, Winston and Candlish, Stewart, 'Determinism and the Ability to do Otherwise'. *Mind* 87, no. 347 (July 1978): 415–20

Newton, Isaac, *The Principia: Mathematical Principles of Natural Philosophy*. CA: University of California Press, 2016.

Nietzsche, Friedrich, *Beyond Good and Evil: Prelude to a Philosophy of the Future*, trans. R. J. Hollingdale. London: Penguin, 2003.

Nietzsche, Friedrich, *Ecce Homo: How One Becomes What One Is*, trans. R. J. Hollingdale. London: Penguin, 2004.

Nietzsche, Friedrich, *The Gay Science*, trans. Walter Kaufmann. New York: Vintage, 1974.

Nietzsche, Friedrich, *On the Genealogy of Morals*, trans. Michael A. Scarpitti. London: Penguin, 2013.

Nietzsche, Friedrich, *Human, All-too-Human: A Book for Free Spirits*, trans. R. J. Hollingdale. Cambridge: Cambridge University Press, 1996.

Ovid, *Metamorphoses*, trans. David Raeburn. London: Penguin, 2004.

Plato, *Euthyphro*, trans. Hugh Tredennick. In *The Last Days of Socrates*. London: Penguin, 1983.

Plato, *Protagoras and Meno*, trans. Adam Beresford. London: Penguin, 2005.

Plato, *The Republic*, trans. Desmond Lee. London: Penguin, 2007.

Plato, *The Seventh Letter*. In *Phaedrus and Letters VII and VIII*, trans. Walter Hamilton. London: Penguin, 1973.

Plato, *Theaetetus*, trans. Robin Waterfield. London: Penguin, 2004.

Reid, Thomas, *Works of Thomas Reid*, Vol. 2. Edinburgh: Maclachlan and Stewart, 1872.

Rousseau, Jean-Jacques, *Discourse on the Origin and the Foundations of Inequality Among Men*. In *The Major Political Writings of Jean-Jacques*

Rousseau, trans. John T. Scott. Chicago: University of Chicago Press, 2012.

Russell, Bertrand, *History of Western Philosophy*. London: Routledge, 1991.

Ryle, Gilbert, *The Concept of Mind*. London: Penguin, 1990.

Sartre, Jean-Paul, *Being and Nothingness*: *An Essay on Phenomenological Ontology*, trans. Hazel E. Barnes. London: Routledge, 2003.

Sartre, Jean-Paul, *In Camera (Behind Closed Doors* or *No Exit)*, trans. Stuart Gilbert. In *In Camera and Other Plays*. London: Penguin, 1990.

Sartre, Jean-Paul, *Existentialism and Humanism*, trans. Philip Mairet. London: Methuen, 1993.

Sartre, Jean-Paul, *Life/Situations: Essays Written and Spoken*, trans. Paul Auster and Lydia Davis. New York: Pantheon, 1977.

Sartre, Jean-Paul, *Notebooks for an Ethics*, trans. David Pellauer. Chicago: University of Chicago Press, 1992.

Sartre, Jean-Paul, *War Diaries: Notebooks from a Phoney War, 1939–1940*, trans. Quintin Hoare. London: Verso, 2000.

Schopenhauer, Arthur, *On the Basis of Morality*, trans. E. F. J. Payne. Indianapolis, IN: Hackett, 2000.

Shakespeare, William, *Henry IV, Part One*. Oxford: Oxford World's Classics, 2008.

Simon, Herbert A., *Models of Man: Social and Rational*. New York: Wiley, 1957.

Singer, Peter, *Practical Ethics*. Cambridge: Cambridge University Press, 1991.

Thomson, Judith Jarvis, 'A Defense of Abortion'. *Philosophy and Public Affairs* 1, no. 1 (Fall 1971): 47–66.

Vanbrugh, John, *The Relapse or Virtue in Danger*. London: Bloomsbury Methuen Drama, 1987.

Warnock, Mary, *Existentialist Ethics*. London: Macmillan, 1967.

Whitehead, Alfred North, *Process and Reality*. New York: Macmillan, 1979.

Whitehead, Alfred North and Bertrand Russell, *Principia Mathematica, Vols 1–3*. Cambridge: Cambridge University Press, 2004.

OTHER MEDIA REFERENCES

Apocalypse Now Redux. American Zoetrope, 2001. Transcript: London: Faber & Faber, 2001.

Celebrity Big Brother. Channel 5, Endemol.

Grand Designs. Channel 4, Boundless Productions.

The Human League. 'Things that Dreams Are Made Of'. Track 1, *Dare*. Virgin-A&M, 1981.

Logan's Run. MGM, 1976.

Monty Python. 'Bruces' Philosophers Song'. Track 16, *Monty Python Sings*. Virgin, 1989.

The Silence of the Lambs. Strong Heart/Demme, 1991.

The Smiths. 'Meat Is Murder'. Track 9, *Meat Is Murder*. Rough Trade, 1985.

FURTHER READING

Atwood, Margaret, *The Handmaid's Tale*. London: Vintage, 2017.

Blackburn, Simon, *Being Good: A Short Introduction to Ethics*. Oxford: Oxford University Press, 2003.

Dent, N. J. H., *The Moral Psychology of the Virtues*. Cambridge: Cambridge University Press, 1984.

Dostoyevsky, Fyodor, *Crime and Punishment*. London: Penguin, 2014.

Holmes, Robert L., *Introduction to Applied Ethics*. London: Bloomsbury, 2018.

Huxley, Aldous, *Brave New World*. London: Vintage, 2007.

Ishiguro, Kazuo, *Never Let Me Go*. London: Faber and Faber, 2010.

MacIntyre, Alasdair, *A Short History of Ethics: A History of Moral Philosophy from the Homeric Age to the 20th Century*. London: Routledge, 2003.

Murdoch, Iris, *The Sovereignty of Good*. London: Routledge, 2001.

Norman, Richard, *The Moral Philosophers: An Introduction to Ethics*. Oxford: Oxford University Press, 2003.

Panza, Richard and Potthast, Adam, *Ethics for Dummies*. Indianapolis, IN: Wiley, 2010.

Wittgenstein, Ludwig, *Lecture on Ethics*. Oxford: Wiley-Blackwell, 2014.

Index